MONEY

The World of Money According To
Gnani Purush Dadashri

Editor : Dr. Niruben Amin

Publisher : **Mr. Ajit C. Patel**
Dada Bhagwan Aradhana Trust
Dada Darshan, 5, Mamta Park Soc,
B/h. Navgujrat College, Usmanpura,
Ahmedabad-380014,
Gujarat, India.
Tel. : +91 79 3983 0100

First Edition : 2000 copies, March, 2005
Second Edition : 2000 copies, November 2006
Third Edition : 3000 copies, March 2009
Fourth Edition : 3000 copies, January 2014

Price : Ultimate Humility (leads to Universal oneness)
and Awareness of "I Don't Know Anything"

Rs. 25.00

Printer : Amba Offset
Basement, Parshwanath Chambers,
Nr. RBI, Usmanpura,
Ahmedabad-380014, Gujarat, India.
Tel. : +91 79 27542964

Trimantra

The Three Mantras that Destroy All Obstacles in Life

Namo Vitaragaya
I bow to the One who is absolutely free from all attachment and abhorrence

Namo Arihantanam
I bow to the living One who has annihilated all internal enemies of anger, pride, deceit and greed

Namo Siddhanam
I bow to the Ones who have attained the state of total and final liberation

Namo Aayariyanam
I bow to the Self-realized masters who impart knowledge of liberation to others

Namo Uvazzayanam
I bow to those who have received the Knowledge of the Self and are helping others attain the same

Namo Loye Savva Sahunam
I bow to all saints everywhere who have received the Knowledge of the Self

Eso Pancha Namukkaro
These five salutations

Savva Pavappanasano
Destroy all demerit karma

Mangalanam cha Savvesim
Of all that is auspicious

Padhamam Havai Mangalam
This is the highest

Om Namo Bhagavate Vasudevaya
I bow to all who have attained the absolute Self in human form

Om Namah Shivaya
I bow to all human beings who have become instruments for salvation of the world

Jai Sat Chit Anand
Awareness of the Eternal is Bliss

NOTE ABOUT THIS TRANSLATION

Gnani Purush Ambalal M. Patel, popularly known as Dadashri or Dada or Dadaji, used to say that it is not possible to exactly translate his satsang on the Science of Self-Realization and the art of worldly interaction, into English. Some of the depth and intent of meaning to be conveyed to the seeker, would be lost. He stressed the importance of learning Gujarati to precisely understand all his teachings.

Dadashri did however grant his blessings to convey his original words to the world through translations in English and other languages. It was his deepest desire and fervor that the suffering human beings of the world attain the living freedom of the wonderful Akram Vignan that expressed within him. He further stated that a day would come when the world would be in awe of the phenomenal powers of this science.

This is an humble attempt to present to the world the essence of the teachings of Dadashri, the Gnani Purush. A lot of care has been taken to preserve the tone and message of his words. This is not a literal translation of his words. Many individuals have worked diligently for this product and we remain deeply thankful to them all.

This is an elementary introduction to the vast new treasure of his teachings. Please note that any errors committed in the translation are entirely those of the translators and for those we request your pardon.

Jai Sat Chit Anand

Introduction to The Gnani

One June evening, in 1958 at around six o'clock, Ambalal Muljibhai Patel, a family man, and a contractor by profession, was sitting on a bench on the busy platform number three at Surat's train station. Surat is a city in south Gujarat, a western state in India. What happened within the next forty-eight minutes was phenomenal. Spontaneous Self-realization occurred within Ambalal M. Patel. During this event, his ego completely melted and from that moment onwards, he became completely detached from all of Ambalal's thoughts, speech, and actions. He became the Lord's living instrument for the salvation of humankind, through the path of knowledge. He called this Lord, 'Dada Bhagwan.' To everyone he met, he would say, "This Lord, Dada Bhagwan is fully manifested within me. He also resides within all living beings. The difference is that within me He is completely expressed and in you, he has yet to manifest."

Who are we? What is God? Who runs this world? What is karma? What is liberation? Etc. All the world's spiritual questions were answered during this event. Thus, nature offered absolute vision to the world through the medium of Shree Ambalal Muljibhai Patel.

Ambalal was born in Tarasali, a suburb of Baroda and was later raised in Bhadran, Gujarat. His wife's name was Hiraba. Although he was a contractor by profession, his life at home and his interactions with everyone around him were exemplary, even prior to his Self-realization. After becoming Self-realized and attaining the state of a Gnani, (The Awakened One, Jnani in Hindi), his body became a 'public charitable trust.'

Throughout his entire life, he lived by the principle that there should not be any commerce in religion, and in all commerce, there must be religion. He also never took money from anyone for his own use. He used the profits from his business to take his devotees for pilgrimages to various parts of India.

5

His words became the foundation for the new, direct, and step-less path to Self-realization called Akram Vignan. Through his divine original scientific experiment (The Gnan Vidhi), he imparted this knowledge to others within two hours. Thousands have received his grace through this process and thousands continue to do so even now. 'Akram' means without steps; an elevator path or a shortcut, whereas 'Kram' means an orderly, step-by-step spiritual path. Akram is now recognized as a direct shortcut to the bliss of the Self.

Who is Dada Bhagwan?

When he explained to others who 'Dada Bhagwan' is, he would say : "What you see here is not 'Dada Bhagwan'. What you see is 'A. M. Patel.' I am a Gnani Purush and 'He' that is manifested within me, is 'Dada Bhagwan'. He is the Lord within. He is within you and everyone else. He has not yet manifested within you, whereas within me he is fully manifested. I myself am not a Bhagwan. I too bow down to Dada Bhagwan within me."

Current link for attaining the knowledge of Self-realization (Atma Gnan)

"I am personally going to impart siddhis (special spiritual powers) to a few people. After I leave, will there not be a need for them? People of future generations will need this path, will they not?" ~ **Dadashri**

Param Pujya Dadashri used to go from town to town, and country to country, to give satsang and impart the knowledge of the Self as well as knowledge of harmonious worldly interaction to all who came to see him. During his final days, in the fall of 1987, he gave his blessing to Dr. Niruben Amin and bestowed his special siddhis upon her, to continue his work. "You will have to become a mother to this whole world, Niruben" He told her as he blessed her. There was no doubt in Dadashri's mind that Niruben was destined to be just that. She had served him with utmost devotion day and night for over twenty years. Dadashri

6

in turn had molded her and prepared her to take on this monumental task.

From the time of Pujya Dadashri's mortal departure on January 2 1988 to her own mortal departure on March 19th 2006, Pujya Niruma as she lovingly came to be called by thousands remained true to her promise to Dadashri to carry on his mission of the world's salvation. She became Dadashri's representative of Akram Vignan and became instrumental in spreading the knowledge of Akram Vignan throughout the world. She also became an exemplary of pure and unconditional love. Thousands of people from all walks of life and from all over the world have attained Self-realization through her and are established in the experience of the pure Soul, while carrying out their worldly duties and obligations. They experience freedom here and now, while living their daily life.

The link of Akram Gnanis now continues with the current spiritual master Pujya Deepakbhai Desai whom Pujya Dadashri had also graced with special siddhis to continue to teach the world about Atma Gnan and Akram Vignan. He was further molded and trained by Pujya Niruma who blessed him to conduct Gnan Vidhi in 2003. Dadashri had said that Deepakbhai will become the decorum that will add splendor to the Lord's reign. Pujya Deepakbhai, in keeping with Dada's and Niruma's tradition travels extensively within India and abroad, giving satsangs and imparting the knowledge of the Self to all who come seeking.

Powerful words in scriptures help the seeker in increasing his desire for liberation. The knowledge of the Self is the final goal of all one's seeking. Without the knowledge of the Self there is no liberation. This knowledge of the Self (Atma Gnan) does not exist in books. It exists in the heart of a Gnani. Hence, the knowledge of the Self can only be acquired by meeting a Gnani. Through the scientific approach of Akram Vignan, even today one can attain Atma Gnan, but it can only occur by meeting a living Atma Gnani and receiving the Atma Gnan. Only a lit candle can light another candle.

❖ ❖ ❖ ❖ ❖

Editorial

In this dangerous time of Kaliyug, it is very difficult to remain ethical and honest in matters of money. This is especially so regarding money that is acquired easily as opposed to money that is earned through ethical practices. The distinction between money earned honestly versus dishonestly is critical especially because it is not easily apparent to the owner. The consequences are as clear as the difference between heaven and hell on earth.

Gnani Purush Dadashri has unfolded the final secrets to liberation for the seeker. In worldly matters he has exposed and presented the final keys to ideal interactions in all matters and especially in matters of money. A balance of both spiritual and worldly interaction is the ideal and fastest way to liberation, like the two wings of the bird. The most critical of worldly interaction is that of money. If this is tainted or impure, no progress can be made spiritually. If this wing is defective then one cannot fly to spiritual heights. The most fortunate of spiritual seekers have been graced with observations of the practical living example of Dadashri's worldly interactions with money. These simple daily life examples and talks of the Gnani Purush are presented here.

By maintaining purity in religion, in business and in his home life, he has shown an extraordinary example of exemplary purity for the whole world. His eternal statement '**Religion must exist in business but business must never exist in religion**', lays down the fundamental requirements of ideal business and spiritual practices.

He has never accepted money from anyone in his life for

even his most crucial expenses. For spiritual discourses, he traveled extensively from villages to towns to cities, regardless of train and airfares, with his own money. Many of his followers offered him thousands of rupees in cash and gold but he never accepted any of it. For those who had an earnest desire to give, he suggested they give for benefit of others, to the temples or the hungry. However, his suggestions only came after he was sure that the money was being offered willingly and within the means of the donor and with the consent of the entire family.

Never before has this world seen a man, in this era of the current time cycle, who had the most ideal worldly interactions and one who was completely free from any attachment. His speech, absolutely pure and free from any attachment flowed from him naturally and spontaneously. Money is a necessity for our livelihood, whether it comes in a form of wages, from one's business or any other means. Despite conducting business, Dadashri has shown us how to walk the path of the Vitarag – the Omniscient Lords, through the essence of his own conduct and experiences.

This world has not seen or heard an example of such an ideal business partner where Dadashri remained as an employee of his business till the end. Even the word 'ideal' does not do justice to this. This is because the concept of ideal has been arrived at based one's individual views and experiences. Dadashri was a wonder of an exceptional ideal presence in this world. This will become apparent as you read this small book.

He maintained an ideal relationship with his business partner, a venture that started when he was 22 years of age. He continued with the same business with his partner's children after the death of his partner, Kantibhai Patel. Although his business of construction was successful and profitable, he drew a salary of only five hundred to six hundred rupees a month, an amount equivalent to the salary of a person with non-metric qualification. The rest of the money was retained in the business in case there was a loss or demand. He maintained this principle during his entire life. He even paid half the cost of the marriage of his partner's children! Where else can one find such an ideal, perfect partner in the world?

Dadashri conducted his business in the most perfect and unparalleled manner and yet his chit and attention remained entirely in the pursuit of the Soul. After his spontaneous Self-realization in 1958, his business continued for many years. He remained as the Self and observed the energies of his mind, speech and body unfold for the salvation of the world. He traveled extensively in small towns and villages. What must be that vision which he attained that allowed him to remain at the zenith of the worldly affairs as well as spirituality!

Money is the prime force in human relationships. Money has been called the eleventh life force.

In his enlightenment, which was a culmination of experiences of many previous lives, Dadashri has the ultimate knowledge of all financial interactions that take place in the world. He has the knowledge of the relationship of the coming and going of money, profit-loss, the hidden principles that govern what a person leaves behind or takes with him when he dies and all principles guiding the slightest dealings with money. These experiences of his life, which have flowed through the medium of his speech, have been compiled in this book. It is our sincere hope that the reader finds this helpful in his efforts to live a life of purity and bliss.

- Dr. Niruben Amin

MONEY

The World of Money According To Gnani Purush Dadashri

[1] Comings And Goings of Laxmiji - the Goddess of wealth (money)

The world considers money and wealth as one of the most important thing in life. People have more love for money because it is needed in everything they do. Love for God cannot exist as long as there is love for money. Love towards money will disappear when a person develops love for God. There can only be love for either Laxmi (Money) or Narayan (God). Love whichever one you want. Laxmi will disappoint you through betrayal. There is a saying "Mandave te randave" – 'That which is built will also be destroyed!' And Narayan, never builds nor destroys. He keeps you happy all the time. He keeps you in a state of liberation.

You will have to understand all this, won't you? How long can you continue with this feebleness of yours? And yet you don't like anxiety. This human life is meant for liberation from anxieties; it is not just for making money. How does a person earn money? Is it through his intellect or his hard work?

Questioner : Both.

Dadashri : If money can be earned through hard work, then these laborers would have lot of money because they work the hardest of all, don't they? And if money could be earned through the intellect, then there are extremely well educated people out there and yet their shoes are all worn out! Earning money is never from the use of the intellect nor is it the fruits of hard labor. It is the reward of one's merit karmas from one's past life. So if you want money, you have to be cautious where merit and demerit karmas are concerned.

Money goes to those with merit karma, whereas hard working people run after money. So from this you should realize that money would only come your way if you have the merit karmas. Hard work will earn you some food and you may have some surplus to get your daughter married, but without merit karma, money will not come your way.

So reality says that if you are a person with a lot of merit karmas, why must you struggle? And if you are not, then why are you struggling? What you are destined to earn in this life cannot be changed.

What is life like for a person with a lot of merit karmas? Let me tell you what even these CEOs have to put up with. How do their wives greet them when they come home after a hard day's work at the office? 'Where have you been, you are two hours late?' Just look at this 'fortunate' (!) ones. Should someone with a lot of merit karma have to put up with this? In reality a truly fortunate one, who has earned a lot of merit karma from last life, does not have to face anything negative in his life. Such people belong to a different breed. From their very youth, they never experience any insults or tough times.

Wherever they go, they are welcomed with a lot of respect. This is how they grow up, whereas other people do nothing but struggle. What does this mean? When a person's merit karma runs out, he is back to where he started. If you do not have the credit of merit karma, then even if you were to go around begging all night, are you likely to get even fifty rupees by the morning? So do not live life struggling helplessly. Be content with what you have.

Your worldly life is the result of no effort. It is totally an outcome of karma of your past life, for which no effort is required. So enjoy it, but know how to enjoy it. Even the Lord concedes that when the basic necessities in life are missing, then it is natural for one to experience suffering. True suffering is, not having any air to breathe, or food to eat. These are the basic necessities in life – without which the body cannot survive. Nowadays people have so many different things available to them and yet they do not enjoy them. They are involved in something else. They do not enjoy what is in front of them. When a wealthy businessman sits to dine, instead of enjoying his meal, he is preoccupied with his business. The fool! He does not even know what he eats. Everything is like this.

This world is a mixture of people who enjoy themselves and those who work very hard. It has a mixture of everything. Those who work very hard have the ego 'I am doing it all'. Those who enjoy themselves have the ego, 'I am enjoying all this'. The one who works hard enjoys the pleasure of doer ship.

A wealthy man once pleaded with me saying, 'Please say something to my son. He does not want to do any work. All he does is enjoys himself and has a good time every day.' I explained to the father, ' It is not worth saying anything. He is only enjoying the fruits of his merit karma. Why should we interfere in his enjoyment?' He replied, ' Is it not important to make him wise?' I told him, 'The wise ones in the world enjoy themselves. The foolish ones waste their wealth. The one who works hard for money is a laborer' Those who work hard derive pleasure from doing so because of their ego. The boss goes to work wearing a long coat so that all the workers would stand and welcome him as he enters the office. His ego is fed. While those who enjoy themselves, care little about power or authority. The truth is to enjoy whatever is yours.

The law of the circulation of money is this: In India as there is an increase in the number of unworthy people; money increases. Where there are forthright and ethical people, the money is lacking. So note that wealth has gone to the unworthy and the undeserving. They have food on their table and do not know how to enjoy it.

There are also the naive and simple people. They are unaffected if they lose money or a valuable thing. They are not concerned with societal status. For such people wealth flows in easily. Wealth does not go to those who have a lot of worldly awareness because these people have a lot of kashay - anger, pride, attachment and greed. The whole daylong they continue to do kashay. The simple ones have no such worldly awareness and are free from these inner turmoil and weaknesses. They do not fuss over things. Wealth flows to them, but they do not know how to make good use of it and it passes away without their awareness.

Whatever money there is in the world today, it is all tainted and wrong. Very little of it is pure and right. There are two kinds of merit karma: One that binds demerit karma and takes a person into a lower life form and the other that binds merit karma which takes a person into a higher life form. The money that results in a birth in a higher life form is very rare in the current era. Where such 'pure and right' money exists, there is continuous inner peace, material comforts and the existence of true religion.

The money of today will bind demerit karma; it is wealth that creates conflicts in the home and outside. Instead it is better to have less of it. At least clashes would not enter the home. Today wherever there is money, there is an atmosphere of conflict. A simple meal of bread and vegetable is better than a gourmet meal with thirty-two dishes. In the current time just one rupee of the right kind will bring tremendous peace and inner satisfaction. Such money creates an atmosphere of harmony in the family and will prompt only spiritual thoughts in everyone.

I once asked a woman from a reputable family in Bombay whether they had any quarrels in their home. She replied, "Every morning we have quarrels for breakfast!" I told her they must be saving a lot of money on food and she replied, "No, we still have to spend money. As we butter the toast, the quarrels go on and so does the breakfast!" What kind of people are these?

If the money is pure and right, then you will always be at peace and your life will be good. Clashes in the homes are caused by entry of impure and wrong money. From a very young age I had decided that as far as possible impure and wrong money must not enter my home. For the past sixty-six years not a trace of impure money has entered my home and that is why there has never been any clashes in my home. We had decided from the very beginning that we would run the household within a certain budget. The business may make hundreds of thousands of rupees but if this Ambalal Patel were to work for someone, how much would he earn? He would earn anywhere between six to seven hundred rupees at the most. Business is a play of merit and demerit karma and so we should spend only the amount I would draw as a salary if I were employed elsewhere. The rest of the money would be retained in the business for unforeseen events like taxes. One never knows when an 'attack' from an income tax authority will come and if all the money is spent, the attack from the tax office will cause you to have a heart attack! Have such attacks not entered all the homes? How can we call this life? What do you think? Is this not a mistake? We need to break this mistake.

Let money flow in naturally. Do not use it as a support. Never rest and think that it will be there forever. Proceed with caution of this awareness so that when it leaves you will not suffer.

Questioner : Describe the fragrance of pure money, please.

Dadashri : Pure money will never bring a trace of stress or tension. There will be enough money in the home. Your mind will be at peace even if someone announces that sugar is going to be rationed starting the next day. Nothing will cause stress or tension to you in the home. The exsisting merit karma effect is such that your actions and speech will be pleasant towards everyone around you. It will never incite worries in you about how you will earn money.

Here what we have all around us is the money of the wrong kind, which will lead to sin and demerit karma. This cannot be called money in the true sense. The thoughts that arise with such money are evil, and of demerit. The thoughts are, ' How can I accumulate a big bank balance?' That is sin.

Some people ask me, 'Did the landlords in the past have

such pure money?' Yes, they did. Their money accumulated naturally. They did not have to accumulate it whereas people today are struggling to accumulate it. The pure money of the past came in naturally, even when they begged the Lord for it not to come. Even when they said they wanted spiritual wealth not material wealth, the money would still flow in their direction. That is the merit karma, which brings pure money.

I never liked this worldly life. Let me tell you about myself. Nothing in this worldly life interested me. If someone gave me money, I found it burdensome, even when the money was mine. I felt a burden when I took my salary, and a burden in taking it home. Before this Gnan (Self-realization), I found everything bothersome.

Questioner : We are so involved in making money in our business that we are not able to turn away from it and we are constantly preoccupied with it.

Dadashri : And even then you are not satisfied. You feel you want to make one million and when you reach that goal, you want to make two, then you think you will stop at five. This does not end.

Even I would have made a decision to make a million. Then I came to the conclusion that life does not give you an extension. If we were given a thousand years instead of a hundred to live, this decision may work. There is no surety of anything in life.

There are two types of authorities: One is an independent authority and the other is dependent authority. It is your independent authority to become a God. To make money is not under your authority. So which is better, to make money or to realize the Self? I know how money comes. If the authority to make money were in one's own hands, then one would even fight for it. But that is not the case and so no matter what you do, you will not accomplish anything. A person once asked me about the nature of money. I told him that money is like sleep. Some people fall asleep the moment they lie down; some toss and turn the whole nightlong and still cannot fall asleep, while some need to take sleeping pills. So money is not under your authority. It is under the authority of some other power, so what is the point in worrying about it and running after it?

Therefore, I tell you that money will not come to you if you go through extreme struggles to acquire it. It simply happens. You are merely an instrument, one of the many evidences when it comes to you. You are merely one of the evidences when you go and return from the court (talking to a lawyer disciple), so is the speech of yours in the trial. All this is not worth paying too much attention to. What is needed happens with the right amount of attention by itself. If you gain this understanding you will be free from all tension.

Currently you have the firm conviction that without you the case in the court will not proceed. This is not so.

When a whole lot of evidences come together, money comes. If you ask a doctor whose father is in the final stages of life in the hospital to do an operation to make him live longer, he will not be able to do so. So this is not under anyone's control. The evidences have come together for the old man to leave this world. I became a Gnani because of scientific circumstantial evidences. And all these billionaires do not become so because of their efforts. They however do believe that it is because of their independent effort and hard work that they are billionaires. 'I became' is the illusion. 'It happened' is knowledge.

Gnani Purush is never under any illusion. He says it as it is, and says it as it happened. I was sitting at Surat station and it happened. The billionaire says, I made millions and I have had three wives. All these you have brought forth with you from your past life. This is nothing but just a belief in your mind that, 'I am doing all this'. This is egoism. What does this egoism do? It plans for your next life, without your knowledge. Thus man creates life after life. He never comes to a life where there is no new life created. If planning stops then liberation is at hand.

There is no being in this world, which does not seek happiness. Everyone seeks eternal bliss, the kind that never leaves. His understanding and belief is that money will bring happiness. But then, the problems and inner turmoil come with it. Eternal bliss and inner turmoil are enemies. They can never exist together. Money is not at fault here. He is the one who is at fault.

All things of this world will one day become unpleasant and unwelcome. The Soul is your own Self. There is no suffering here. The worldly existence is such that a time arrives when even money becomes burdensome. One worries about how to store and distribute it.

So in life there is suffering. Suffering with money, suffering without money, suffering as a pauper, suffering as a prime minister, suffering as widow, suffering as a wife, suffering even as a mistress, suffering, suffering, suffering. Why are all these big businessmen of Ahmedabad suffering? What is the cause?

Questioner : They are discontent and unhappy.

Dadashri : There never was any happiness in this work of theirs. Where is the happiness? This is the illusion. It is like a drunken man lying on the street with a hand in the cold contents of a gutter. He is under the inebriation and false belief of happiness. When the effect of the alcohol wears off he will feel the pain. This is all nothing but a gutter.

There is no happiness in the worldly life whatsoever. There can never be happiness in it at all because if there were, then the city of Bombay would not be the way it is today. There is no happiness at all. It is all an illusion of happiness and it is only a temporary adjustment.

There is no need to carry a burden over money. When the bank balance grows he breathes a sigh of satisfaction and when there is a deficit he becomes sad and unhappy. There is nothing in this world worth breathing a sigh of satisfaction, because everything is temporary.

What makes people suffer? A man once came to me and said, 'I have no money in the bank. I am completely broke and bankrupt'. I asked him, 'How much debt did you have?' He told me he did not have any debt. That is not bankruptcy! He had a few thousand rupees in the bank. Then I asked him, ' Do you have a wife?' He answered 'I can't sell my wife'. I told him, ' No you can't, but you have two eyes. Would you like to sell them for two hundred thousand rupees?' Your eyes, your hands, your feet, your brain; all this is your wealth. Don't disregard this wealth of yours. Even without a penny in the bank you are a billionaire. Try and sell each of these assets of yours. You will not sell your two hands. This is your endless wealth. Consider all this as your wealth and be content. Money may come or not. It does not matter whether a person has money or not as long as he gets food to eat.

Questioner : What should we do when times are tough and there is no money coming in?

Dadashri : When rain does not fall for an entire year, the farmers cry and say that they are ruined. The rains return the next year and their financial position improves. So when times are tough, patience is necessary. Decrease your expenses and with hard work and frugal economy pass your time. Do this only during the tough period. When the going is good you do not have to do anything.

At such difficult times, give this body the necessary food. It does not demand anything else. Also if needed, recite these three mantras, the Trimantra, for an hour daily. When you do this, your life situation will improve. For thousands of people, the difficulties and obstructions in life have been eliminated by the name 'Dada Bhagwan', recited with understanding.

What is the nature of money? Money means pain in earning, pain in protecting, pain in spending. When a hundred thousand rupees arrive at home, the pain of protecting it begins. The search for the bank that will not disappear starts, and then some relatives and friends come to know about it and they pester you for loans and gifts. My buddy, do you not have this much trust for me? All I want is a mere ten thousand, and you have to give when you are pestered enough. So the pain exists when there is excess and when there is scarcity. It is best when it is just normal. Otherwise there is pain when spending.

People do not know how to take care of money nor do they know how to enjoy it. They complain about how expensive things are even while they are enjoying them. The fools! Why not enjoy what you have peacefully? People have to work to make money in an environment that makes them miserable. Many people will not return the money they owe, so there is suffering in earning money and suffering in safekeeping it also. Even when extreme care is taken in protecting the money in the bank, it does not remain there. A bank account means credit and debit, coming and going. Anguish results when money leaves.

Many have become rich by evading income taxes. They have hidden millions from the government. They do not know that this money will leave someday. When the fines and demands come from the income tax department, where will they go? This is all a trap, nothing else. These persons who have risen up this way carry so much danger with them, but are unaware of it. They are all involved in schemes to avoid income taxes all day and this meditation of theirs is indeed the return ticket to an animal life form.

Life of making money is like that of an ox running circles around the stone mill to crush castor oil seeds. The farmer gives a bunch of fodder for the toil to the ox, and here the wife gives the plate of food for the toil of the day. No difference.

These big shots of Ahmedabad are owners of two or more cotton mills, yet their suffering is beyond description here. They are under constant tension of these mills not performing or shutting down. They passed in the educational school well, but have failed in the school of life. This is because they have adopted the best foolishness. Dishonesty is the best foolishness. There has to be a limit to foolishness, do you not think so? Yet here they have crossed the limit.

I have analyzed the nature of money from all aspects. How much money can a person accumulate? I came to the conclusion that no one has ever managed to remain the richest person in the world. People used to say that Ford was the richest man, but a few years later we heard that someone else was. What is the point to all this? The horse that wins the race gets the first prize, the second and third horse will get some recognition, but what about the horse that comes fourth? He just runs the race in vain, foaming at the mouth. I said 'Why do I enter this race course?' Why should one have to foam at the mouth unnecessarily? People enter this race to come first but instead they all lose the race. No body cares for these late arrivals.

Money is limited whereas people's demands are not.

Some people have an obsession for sex, some for pride, status and recognition; there are so many different types of obsessions. Some people are obsessed with money. They are constantly preoccupied with thoughts of money and ways of accumulating it. Preoccupation with money is a heavy obsession.

Questioner : But one cannot do without money.

Dadashree: Yes, you cannot do without it but people do not know how money comes to them and so they keep running after it. Money is like perspiration. It comes like perspiration. Some people perspire profusely while others perspire very little. Just as sweating is inevitable, so is the coming of money.

I never cared for money from the very beginning. I started business at the age of twenty-two and if someone came to visit me, they would have no knowledge about how my business was faring but I would ask them if they were having any financial difficulties.

It is dangerous to even have thoughts about money, so you can imagine how dangerous it is to run after and revere it.

Man can only go after one thing, either money or the Soul. It is not possible for a person to be attentive in two places at the same time. Either his attention is on money or it is on the Self. The focus of the worldly self can only be in one place. So what is one to do?

Once I met a wealthy man. He was a millionaire. He was fifteen years older than I but he would sit next to me. I asked him how was it that his children wore shirts and pants, but he wore a dhoti, which barely covered his knees! He looked half naked even when going to the temple! In such a short dhoti, it appeared as if he was draped in a loincloth, wearing a short sleeve shirt and a white cap rushing to the temple to do darshan. I told him it appeared to me that he was going to take all his wealth with him when he dies. He told me it was not possible to do such a thing. I told him we the Patels are not as clever as the Jains and that possibly the Jains must have found a way to do so. He told me no one could take anything with him or her when they die. When I told his son about our conversation, his son exclaimed it was a good thing no one could do so otherwise his dad would take out a loan of three million rupees and leave the debt for him to repay. He told me his dad is so shrewd that it would ruin him.

Questioner : Many big businessmen of Bombay accumulate money taken under the table, what effect will this bring on them?

Dadashri : It binds karmas. Both the black money and the white money bind karmas. Good money or bad money, all money binds karma. Karmas are being bound constantly. Until a person attains Self-realization, he or she continues to bind karmas. With black money, one binds bad karma and will spend a life in the animal kingdom.

Questioner : Why are people who run after money never satisfied?

Dadashri : If you tell someone to be content, he will retort and say the same thing to you and even ask why you are so discontent. Contentment is not something that can be acquired, even when a person wants to be. Contentment is attained through knowledge and worldly experience. It happens naturally and is directly proportional to the level of one's knowledge. It is not something that will happen by doing anything. It is an effect, a result. Your grade will depend upon how well you write your examination. The examination was given in the past life. The result is the knowledge of this life. In the same way, your contentment will be as good as your knowledge in this life. It is for this contentment that people work so hard. However, what we see is the opposite. Even when they go to the latrine, they are performing two tasks. They shave their faces while sitting on the latrine. They have so much greed and are in such a hurry to make money. This is called the Indian puzzle.

One lawyer shaves as he sits on the toilet and his wife tells me that he does not even talk to her. He has become so isolated. He is stuck in just one corner and he is constantly on the run. He makes money and he squanders it in those other useless places. He milks a cow and feeds the milk to a donkey.

In this day and age of kaliyug (the fifth era of the time cycle), a person ruins his life by becoming greedy for money. By having aartadhyan (adverse internal meditation causing harm to ones own self) and raudradhyaan (adverse internal meditation implicating and causing hurt to others) people lose their right to be born as humans again. In their past life these very people have enjoyed the luxuries of grand kingdoms and royalty. They were never such beggars, but in this day and age their minds have become beggarly. Their mind wants this and that! Otherwise a person whose mind is fulfilled will walk around like a king, even if he has nothing. Money is such a thing that it turns one's vision towards greed. Money increases vengeance and negative passions. The further you can stay away from money, the better it is for you. And if it is spent, it is better spent towards a noble cause.

The money that is going to flow in cannot be changed. This is not going to be changed whether one becomes religious or evil. If he falls into evil deeds, it will be a waste of money and invite more suffering. If he turns religious and spends the money rightly, he will invite happiness and this may show him the path to liberation. The amount of money will not change.

To delve constantly about making money is a bad habit. It is like giving a daily steam bath to a person with daily fever. There is an initial temporary relief, so he becomes habituated to it. The fever will come down, but the cause of the fever has not been treated so that it returns every day. Likewise, running after money is futile.

Money is a by-product. Do you worry whether your arms or legs will remain functional? No. Why not? Do we not need our limbs? We do, but it is not something we have to think about. In the same manner there is no need to think about money. If your arm hurts, you have to think about getting treatment for it but you do not have to worry about it. You should never be exclusively preoccupied with money. When you devote too much attention to money, you miss out on other important things in life. And it is not just preoccupation with money that is forbidden, but also preoccupation with women. If you become obsessed with women, you will become like a woman. If you become obsessed with money, then you will become restless. Money roams and so will you. One should never become obsessed with money. It is the highest raudradhyana (- adverse internal meditation that hurts the person having it and also others around). It is not artadhyana (adverse meditation hurting only the person having it), because although a person may have food and everything else in his home, he still has expectations of more wealth. When a person runs after money, other people are deprived of their share of the wealth. Do not do anything that will create shortage for others. Do not break the proportion of the distribution of wealth in a way that will cause shortage for others. Otherwise you will be liable for it. If money comes to you spontaneously, then you are not liable. You may get five thousand or even fifty thousand rupees spontaneously, but once it comes to you, you cannot detain it or obstruct it from leaving. What is the natural law of money? It says, 'Do not detain and hoard me. Circulate me. Give away as much as comes your way'.

Obstacles to money will remain as long as you harbor the desire to earn it. When you become inattentive to money, it will come to you in abundance.

Is it not necessary to eat food? Is it not necessary to go to the toilet? Similarly money is necessary. Just as you are able to go to the bathroom without having to think about it, so will money come to you without you thinking about it.

A wealthy landowner once came to me. He wanted to know how much wealth a person should accumulate. He told me he had about a thousand acres of land, a bungalow, two cars and a sizable bank balance. He wanted to know how much he should keep. I told him that every person should assess their needs based on what luxury he had at the time of his birth. That is the exact principle for happiness. Everything else falls in the category of excessiveness. Anything in excess is poisonous, and invites misery.

Each person finds happiness in his or her own home. A man living in a hut will not find happiness in a bungalow and a man living in a bungalow will not find happiness in a hut. The reason behind this is what people bring forth within their 'receptacle' of intellect (buddhi no ashay) from their past life. People will find or come across whatever they have brought forth within their receptacle of intellect. Whatever people bring forth in their receptacle of intellect can be divided in two parts: effects of merit karma and effects of demerit karma. If we divide up what people fill in their receptacle of intellect, most of it is to acquire material wealth and happiness and they use up their merit karma in order to acquire these two things, leaving them with only a very small amount to acquire spirituality.

A person brings forth in his receptacle of intellect that he wants to acquire a lot of money. He expends a lot of his merit karma in the process and gets his desired wealth. Another person does the same but instead of effects of merit karma, he is faced with effects of his demerit karma, consequently he remains broke despite working very hard. These accounts are very exact and precise and no one can change that. And yet these foolish people believe the wealth they have acquired is through their own efforts. They do not realize that they have expended their merit karma in the process and that too, on the wrong path. Instead why not turn around the receptacle of your intellect; if you are to have one, the only thing worth having in it is spirituality and nothing materialistic. The effect of merit karma has to be spent on religion and not on useless material things like cars, radios, televisions etc. Place the desire to know the Self, and the desire to do good for others, as the only things in your receptacle, which carries forth into the next life. Whatever has come your way at the moment, let it be, but from now on change this.

I have brought forth in my receptacle of intellect, a one hundred percent intention for the Soul and the salvation of the world. My merit karma has not been spent anywhere else, and especially not for any material things.

Those who have met me and have attained Gnan, were able to do so because they had allocated some two to five percent of their merit karma for this. That is why they were able to meet me. Whereas I spent one hundred percent for the Self and that is why I have been granted the certificate of 'No Objection' for religion from all sides.

If someone were to tell me that no matter what he does, he keeps running into a loss, I would tell him that it is because his demerit karma is in operation. I will tell him not to borrow any money from anyone, because that money is unlikely to help him. He will lose it. I tell him to sit at home, study his favorite scripture and pray to God.

People continue to bind demerit karma but when the effect of these karma manifest, they will suffer a lot. These effects will completely shake them. They will feel as if they are standing on burning coal. In the same token they will realize how sweet the rewards are if they bind merit karma. So beware! Whatever karma you bind, think before you do so and realize what kind of effect such karma will bring forth when they mature. Maintain extreme vigilance during the charging of karma. You are binding demerit karma when you increase your wealth by cheating others of their money; when you do this remember at the time that the effect of such karma is inevitable. And even if you deposit that money in the bank, it will eventually go away. That wealth too, is certain to dissipate. But in the process of trying to accumulate that wealth, you create raudradhyan, which will not only make you suffer immediately but also later when the result of demerit karma unfold. At that time you will have a lot of suffering.

What does nature say? It is not concerned with how much money you spend, it is only concerned with the internal state of pain and pleasure. Nature only keeps account of how much pain or pleasure is derived. A person enjoys happiness even when there is no money whatsoever, and another suffers deeply when there is plenty of money. Therefore pleasure and pain are not dependent on money.

Those who make relatively little money are in peace; they do not have any problems. They even have time to go to the temple and do darshan of the Lord. But for those who are engrossed in trying to increase their money, there is a problem when they earn a million rupees, and when they incur a loss of fifty thousand rupees, they immediately experience distress and suffering. You foolish people! Just deduct the fifty thousand from the million that you have. But no! That would reduce the original sum earned. What are you defining as your original sum? The sum you lost, carried away with it responsibility on your part, so do not complain when that sum decreases. But instead you feel happy when that sum increases and what happens when that sum decreases? Pain. The real sum is within you; the real wealth is within you. Why then do you frantically go around setting yourself up for a heart attack and risk loosing this real sum? If you were to die of a heart attack, will you not lose this sum, the Self?

A father gives his son a million rupees and then decides to embark on a spiritual path. The son squanders the money away, drinking, eating non-vegetarian food, gambling in the stock market, and enjoying himself. The reason behind this is that any money acquired through improper means will never remain; it will leave. Alas today not even honest money earned through earnest means remains with those who earn it, so how is dishonest money to remain? So you will need money that comes from your merit karma, pure money. This occurs when money is gained through honest and clear intentions. Only the wealth from such a source will give you happiness. Otherwise, the impure money of demerit karma will make you suffer even as it leaves, and will bind demerit karma in the process.

This worldly life is such that one cannot afford to live in it, not even for a minute. Even when a person has tremendous merit karma, there is so much internal suffering that it is unbearable. He cannot contain his suffering. He is surrounded by the finest of circumstances and yet there is burning within, an internal suffering. How can this suffering be allayed? Eventually even his merit karmas are exhausted. What is the principle of this world? It is that when all the merit karmas become depleted, the effect of demerit karma begins. As it is, a person already has a lot of internal suffering, but what will become of him when he is surrounded by externally induced suffering? Therefore, be aware! That is what the Lord says.

The nature of everything around is intake and output, filling and emptying (puran and galan). Whatever fills, eventually drains. If it did not drain, there would be a problem. It is because there is an out flow that you are able to eat again. When you inhale it is an in flow and when you exhale it is an out flow. The intrinsic nature of everything is to flow in and out and that is why I have made the discovery that there should be neither feast nor famine as far as money is concerned. For me, always there is neither too much nor too little of wealth. Those with too little will shrink away and those with excess will bloat up. Excess means that money will last for two to three years. It is better to have wealth which is flowing otherwise it will bring suffering.

I have never had too little money, nor has there been an excess amount of money. Before the sum of saving approached a hundred thousand there would be an emergency in the business and it would be spent. That is why money never accumulated to the point of overflow nor was there ever any shortage.

Questioner : Why is there a shortage of money?

Dadashree: Money does not come because of stealing. Where there is no stealing through the mind, speech or body, money is abundant. Stealing is an obstacle to wealth. Deception and money are enemies. When a person stops stealing overtly he will take birth in a noble family. Deception is subtle stealing and that is regarded as severe raudradhyan, the consequence of which is a life in hell. There should be absolutely no deception. A shopkeeper may take pleasure in selling adulterated goods; he tells his customers that his goods are pure and of the highest quality, and when you question him about his tactics, he insists and says: 'This is the only way to do business' – that is deception. A person who has the desire to be honest can say to his customers, 'My wish is to sell only the best but this is what my goods are like so take them if you want'. By merely stating this, he is freed from any liability.

People remain honest as long as they do not get the taste of black money. Once they start dealing with black money dishonesty creeps in.

Questioner : How much money should one earn?

Dadashri : There is no such rule. Do you worry about

how much water you will get for your shower every morning? Similarly you should not think about money. Everything is pre-ordained; whether you get one or two buckets of water, it has already been decided. No one is able to add or take away from this. Make all efforts to earn money through your mind, speech and body, but do not hold any desire for it. Money is a bank balance; will you not get it if it is meant to be for you? Desire for money will further delay the money coming to you. Nor should you shun money. If you were to say, 'I don't want any money', that too is a great offence. There should be neither rejection nor desire for money. One should only have respect for money. Money will come when the time is right. Desire for it will create obstacles for its arrival. Laxmiji (the Goddess of wealth) says: "Whatever the time and circumstances you find yourself, accept that situation for that time and from time to time I will send to you whatever is due to you. Whatever is due to you will come to you at its preordained time; however do not harbor a desire for me. I will send with interest what is rightfully yours. Those who do not harbor desire, to them I send their money on time'. What else does Laxmiji say? She says that if a person wants liberation, then he may take only the money that is his by right; he must not cheat or deceive anyone for money.

Whenever I meet Laxmiji, I tell her: 'My address is house number six, in Mamanipoda, Baroda. Whenever it is convenient for you, grace us with a visit and leave whenever you please. That is your home and you are welcome there.' This is what I tell her. I never forsake courtesy.

The other point is that you can never shun or reject Laxmi. Many people say: "I do not need money. I do not even touch money'. It is fine if they do not touch money, but when they speak this way and mean what they say from within, it is very dangerous. They will wander for many lives to come without any money. Laxmi is vitaraag (without attachment). Money is inanimate. For that matter you should never shun anything either; whether it is animate or inanimate, because by doing so you will not encounter it again. I may say that I am aparigrahi (one who is not attached to material things), but I will never say that I will never touch money. Money is the center of all worldly interactions. All these deities have been organized to support the rules and principles of scientific circumstantial evidences, called vyavasthit. So you should never reject anything.

It is not money, but ignorance that needs to be renounced. Many people have contempt towards money. Whatever you have contempt towards, will never come your way. Disinterest or indifference for money in the absence of any real interest (Soul) is the worst kind of madness.

I maintain indifference in matters of worldly life and absolute interest in matters of the Soul. There has to be both. Indifference for the worldly matters and interest for the Soul is needed for liberation. So gladly welcome each and every circumstance that comes your way.

Let me explain to you the nature of black market money. When there is flooding due to a heavy rainfall and the water enters your home through your front yard, you feel glad that the water is coming to you without any effort, but when that water drains away, it will leave behind a sludge of mud. You will have a hard time getting rid of that mud. Black money is like the water of the flood. It will sting you all over before it leaves. This is why I have to caution all the wealthy businessmen.

Money will not leave as long as you do not indulge in deceptive business tactics. Deceptive business practice is the cause of money leaving your home.

The current time is such that people are preoccupied with how they can acquire and enjoy more wealth and in wanting this they do not care whether the money rightfully belong to them or not. They are blinded by their greed. They can only look for other things if they become free from their preoccupation with cheating others, making a profit by selling adulterated goods and enjoying adulterous relationships. Happiness does not lie in such practices. Happiness is to be found when you make your spiritual path as your main production. All worldly gains are a by-product of such a production. You have acquired this body because of something you did in your previous life. You have acquired material wealth, a wife, a bungalow etc. All this is a by-production. If all these things were attainable through only hard work, then all the laborers would also have the same, but it is not so. People today have misunderstood this and that is why they have started factories of 'by-production'. Effort made in the path of liberation is considered the 'main production'. You should acquire liberation from the 'Gnani Purush', after which the worldly 'by-production' will automatically come to you, free of cost. You have wasted so many lives for this 'by-production'. Just once come and get your liberation so that your endless wanderings and misery comes to an end.

Instead of worldly happiness, you should have happiness that is beyond this world, spiritual happiness; such happiness is one that will make you content. Worldly happiness, on the contrary, increases restlessness, and is temporary. If a person makes a sale of fifty thousand rupees, he will count and recount his money and his mind becomes exhausted in counting. People's minds have become so agitated that they do not even like to eat. I too have experienced such sales and I have observed what it does to the mind. This is not something that is outside my own experience. I myself have swum through this very ocean and gone across. So I understand what you are going through. The more money you make the more restless you become and the mind becomes dull and you do not remember anything. You are in a constant state of agitation. People keep counting their bills; the bills are left behind and the counter passes on. Money says to us, 'Understand this much if you want: you will move on and we will stay behind'. Therefore do not create any animosity with it. Invite money to come to you because you need it. We have a need for everything. But people become obsessed with it. However you have no choice but count it anyway. There are a few businessmen who delegate the bookkeeping, counting and safekeeping of money to their clerks. They instruct their clerks not to disturb them when they are dinning. They tell their clerks to count the money on their own as they take the money in and out of the safe. They will not interfere with their assistants. There are such men around. In the whole of India, there are a handful of such men who remain completely unaffected. They are like me. I never count money. What interference! I have not handled money for the last twenty years and that is why I am filled with bliss.

There is no denying that as long as there are monetary interactions, there is a need for it. But one cannot become preoccupied with it. One can however become preoccupied with the Lord. If you only pursue money (Laxmi), then Narayan (God) will be enraged. Do we not have temples of Laxmi-Narayan? Is Laxmiji an ordinary thing?

Whatever enjoyment you get from earning money, you should also experience the same enjoyment whilst spending it. But instead people keep commenting on how much money gets spent away.

You should never be engrossed with the thought that your money will be spent away. At whatever time the money goes, that is correct and that is why it has been said that money should be spent because in doing so people will lessen their tendencies of greed and consequently will be able to give over and over again.

The Lord has said that you should not keep an account of your money. If you have some knowledge of what the future holds, do keep an account. And if you want to keep an account then keep the account that guarantees that one day you will not be around in this world.

The law of money is such that it will linger for some time and then it will leave, and leave it will. Money will wander around, whether it will bring you profit, loss or interest, but it will wander. It will not remain in one place forever. Money by nature is restless. People rise to the top with their money but when they get there, they find it very difficult. They feel trapped and it is difficult for them to come back down. They climb to the top with a lot of enthusiasm but while coming down their predicament is like the cat that forces its face into a jar of milk. What happens to that kitten when it wants to come out? This is the same predicament.

These grains will lose their potential to grow into new crops in three to five years. Likewise money that does not circulate becomes useless.

The wealth of past days was such that it would remain within a family for up to five generations. But today it will not last even for one generation. It comes within one's lifetime and leaves while he is living. What kind of wealth is this? This wealth is such that it comes because of one's merit karma but it binds demerit karma (papa-anubandhi-punya) as it leaves. There is very little of it, which binds merit karma (punya-anubandhi-punya); this is the wealth that motivates you to come here to meet the Gnani Purush and make you spend money on this path of Akram Vignan. That wealth will flow on a worthy path, otherwise it will all squander away. Everything will drain away into the gutter. These children of yours are enjoying the money. You tell them they are enjoying your money but they will tell you they are enjoying their share and therefore it is not yours. When they say this, this is the same as money going down the gutter.

This life is worth living only if you understand and come to know the true nature of this world. If you understand it exactly the way it is, then there would be no worries or external problems. Then you would feel that life is worth living!

[2] The Intricacy Of Money Exchange

Wealth comes your way when you give help to others, not otherwise. Wealth comes to those who have the desire to give. It comes to those who believe in giving; those who know-ingly allow others to cheat them and those who spend money with a big heart. It may appear that it has gone away, but it will return there only.

You will need merit karma in order to earn money. The intellect on the contrary will bind demerit karma. If you try to earn money through your intellect, you will bind demerit karma. I have no intellect and therefore I bind no demerit karma. I do not have even one percent of intellect.

I am kind and empathetic. On a rare occasion when I set out to collect money owed to my business, I would return actu-ally giving them more. As such I never set out to collect money, but when I did and if that person was experiencing difficulties, I ended up giving him more. I would give away the money in my pocket that I needed for my expenses. And the next day I found myself in difficulty. This is how my life has been.

Questioner : Does a person's attachment to money not increase as his money increases? The more the money, the greater the intoxication, is it not so?

Dadashri : Everything creates intoxication. There is no problem with an increase in money as long as one does not become intoxicated with it. But once a person's ego increases as a result of wealth, he becomes intoxicated, he moves around in that pride! He calls others poor. Who are you to call others poor? You big aristocrat! There is no telling when a person will be faced with poverty. It is exactly as you say. Intoxication of money is inevitable.

People of this world are chasing money their entire life. I have yet to see a man who is satisfied with his money. Then where did it all go?

Everything is happening in a haphazard manner where money is concerned. People have not understood a single word of religion and yet everything goes on. And yet when people fall into difficulties, they do not know how to get out. They jump with joy when the dollars come piling in but when they are faced with difficulties, they have no clue about what to do and instead they bind demerit karma over and over again. True religion is to know how to pass the time during such difficulties and not bind any demerit karma.

It is a natural principle of this world that there is a sunrise and a sunset. In the same manner wealth will continue to increase as past karmas come into fruition. It will increase in every aspect, cars, bungalows, jewelry etc. But when it changes, it will continue to disperse. First it will accumulate and then it will disperse. At the time when it disperses, you should remain calm. That is the highest inner endeavor (purusharth).

It is purusharth to continue living with your brother who refuses to return your fifty thousand dollars and continues to insult you. Knowing how to conduct your self during this time is your purusharth.

It is purusharth when you know how to conduct yourself if a servant steals goods worth ten thousand dollars from your office. If you fail at this time, you will ruin your next life.

Questioner : In Aptavani you have said that when one begs for two thousand dollars from someone, one is selling his pride and ego. Please explain.

Dadashri : Yes, he sold his pride and ego. If he sells his ego, we should buy it. I have spent my entire life buying egos. You should buy ego.

Questioner : What does that mean Dada?

Dadashri : If someone comes asking you for two thousand dollars don't you think he is embarrassed and feels ashamed in doing so?

Questioner : Yes.

Dadashri : When he asks you for money, he is risking embarrassment and shame and selling his ego to you. You should buy his ego, if you have the money.

Do you think it feels good to ask for money? Does it feel good to ask even your uncle? Why not? You don't like asking even a close friend for money. Not even from your father.

People do not like to stretch out their hand.

Questioner : We buy their ego, but of what use is it to us?

Dadashri : Oh ho ho! When you buy his ego, whatever strength he has within him will manifest within you. The poor fellow has come to you to sell his ego.

Questioner : Is it a wrong doing, will it bind demerit karma to refuse to give money to a beggar who is robust and healthy?

Dadashri : There is no problem if you do not give, but you must never rebuke him asking him why he is begging when he has such good health. You can always tell him that you are not able to give.

You should never utter words that hurt others. Keep your speech such that it will give happiness to others. Your speech is the greatest wealth you have. The other wealth may or may not last but the wealth of your speech will be with you forever. The good words you utter will impart happiness to the other person. There is no problem if you do not give him any money, but at least speak kindly to him.

You become a beggar of the world if you build a majestic bungalow and a king of the world with a small bungalow. Material prosperity is a counterbalance to spiritual prosperity. This is because this entire world is the material world and when the material world increases, the soul (the unrealized self) attached to that material world becomes small. When the material world attached to the relative self decreases, internal awareness increases as the soul expresses. Therefore all worldly sorrows are a vitamin for the soul and worldly happiness is the vitamin for the body.

What is the nature of money? It is unsteady and transitory. Make good use of it so that you do not misuse it. Do not keep it stagnant, because by nature there are many different types of money. One is flowing! Liquid cash is all movable wealth. The immovable wealth is things like homes, property etc. Of the two, the immovable wealth will last longer while the liquid wealth will disappear! So what is the nature of cash? It does not last more than ten years. The nature of gold is that it will last forty to fifty years and the immovable wealth, real estate, will last up to a hundred years. Therefore the fixed period is different for each, but ultimately all of it will go. You will have to understand all this before you do anything. The Vaniks, the business class in India used to invest twenty five percent of their wealth in their business; twenty five percent for interest; twenty five percent in gold and twenty percent in real estate. This is how they organized their wealth. They are very astute people. The young members in the family are not taught this rule of money conservation. How can this be done when there is no money left?

Money is such that it always leaves in the eleventh year. It will last for ten years. This applies to honest money! Honest money leaves in the eleventh year! There is no telling when the money obtained through dishonest means will leave or what harm it will bring.

Questioner : Which is better, buying gold or speculating in the stock market?

Dadashri : You should never get involved in the stock market. That place is only for shrewd players and professional money managers. Others get roasted in the middle! Only the shrewd people benefit from it. A few people get together and fix the price and others get crushed in the middle! These shrewd people benefit and the small ordinary players pay the price! That is a full time business. The middlemen, the brokers make their living by getting ordinary people involved. When a relative of mine asked me about investing in the stock market, I advised him not to.

Questioner : Dada, the American mahatmas are asking whether they should take whatever savings they have accumulated and go to India. They are especially concerned about their children. The children do not get the right upbringing and environment here in America. Please tell us how much money we need for living in India because here there is no such limit.

Dadashri : Yes, that is true. If you want to start work in India then it will be necessary for you to bring in some money so that you would not need to borrow that money and pay interest on it in India. No one will lend you the money over there, except a bank. So it is better for you to keep some money aside. You have no choice but do business to make money in India. You will also have to meet expenses there. But there your children will blossom. Here you find dollars but there are problems with raising children.

In America, my mahatmas would take me to the large shopping malls. 'Let us go Dadaji', they would say. Even the mall itself is amazed that I am not enticed with anything it has to offer. It would salute me with reverence again and again knowing that nothing it has to offer tempts me. Nothing in the store would catch my eye. I will look at everything but I would not be tempted with anything. What use do I have for anything? There is nothing that has any use for me. You get tempted just by looking, do you not?

Questioner : We have to buy the things, which are necessary.

Dadashri : Yes, but nothing catches my eye. The store

would bow to me because never before had such a person entered it. There is neither temptation nor rejection. There is neither attachment nor abhorrence. Just the pure vitarag, the unattached One, stands in front of you.

One mahatma, asked me whether he should continue investing in the stock market or stop. I told him to stop. I told him to take out whatever money he made so far, but he should now stop. Otherwise it would make no difference in him coming over to America. He would find himself where he was before. He would have to return home with a blank slate.

One starts making money by lending money with interest. One who does so is worse than Muslim in matters of money. A real Muslim never charges interest. There is no need to charge interest because there is no value to the interest. Only God knows what happens to a man who charges interest. It is fine if you keep your money in the bank or if you loan it at reasonable interest to someone, but when you become preoccupied with the greed of eighteen to twenty four percent interest, there is no telling what will become of you. Such is the state of people in.

There is no harm in charging reasonable interest but people have made a business of charging interest. Their entire business is based on charging interest. What should you do instead? Whoever you lend the money to, tell them they will have to pay you interest at the same rate as the bank. However, if that person has absolutely no money at all, no capital or interest to pay, then you should remain silent. You should not do anything that would hurt him. Here you should just take it for granted that you have lost your money. What would you do if your money fell in the ocean?

Questioner : If the government imposes above normal

taxes, then people will steal, and hide their income to make it more bearable. Is that wrong?

Dadashri : Tax is the best instrument to lessen greed. A greedy person will not be satisfied even if he makes fifty million rupees; his greed is never satisfied even when he dies. So when he is taxed in this way, again and again, his greed will be curbed a little, so it is a good thing. The income tax code of the government is fair. Is it not? No taxes are imposed on earnings below fifteen thousand. They grant people fifteen thousand, so that their families do not have problems and can enjoy their earnings. Small families are not taxed heavily, even in Africa.

Questioner : Why is it that people who worship the Lord are poor and unhappy?

Dadashri : Those who are doing bhakti and worship of the Lord are not necessarily unhappy. Some amongst them may appear to you that way. It is precisely because people have done bhakti in their past life that they now have their wealth of bungalows and cars. It is not possible for them to be unhappy because they do bhakti , but their unhappiness in this life is the result of their karmic account from their past life. The bhakti they do now is their new account, the results of which will be realized in their next life. Do you understand? Whatever they deposited in their account from the past is what they are facing right now. The results of the good deeds they perform now are yet to come. Do you understand?

Questioner : What should one do in order to attain peace of mind? Should we take care of the needy, the weak and the poor or should we pray to god? Or give to charity? What should we do?

Dadashri : If you want peace of mind then you should

give what you have to others. Tomorrow bring a bucket of ice cream and feed everyone and tell me about the happiness you feel at the time. These pigeons jump with joy even before you throw the grains to them and when you throw the grains to them, you are giving away something of yours, at the time observe the joy you feel within. If a person falls down and breaks his leg and is bleeding and you tear off a piece of your dhoti to make a bandage for him, you will feel tremendous joy within.

How are the boys and girls of today able to get married? It is like this: parents will spend more money for the daughters; the daughters bring with them account from their past life which makes the parents save the money aside for them. But the father proudly boasts, 'In those days I spent seventy thousand rupees for my daughter's marriage!' Now what has he really done, when in the first place it was the daughter's money that was in the bank all along? He merely has the 'power of attorney'. What if the daughter only brought forward in her account the sum of three thousand rupees? He will remain quiet in her wedding; keep a low profile in everything, including his business. The daughter will get married using only the three thousand because that was all that she had brought with her in her account.

The money really belongs to the children. All we do is save and deposit the money in the bank for them; only the management of their money is in our hands.

Many people say they will pay back their debts by hook or by crook. That is sheer egoism. All you have to do is maintain an unwavering internal resolve that you want to return the money you borrowed, and you will be able to do so. I have observed that people, who take money only after making the decision that they want to repay it, have ideal worldly interactions. Surely there must be some firm decision from the very beginning and if an accident were to occur afterwards, that is a different matter but there must be some intention to begin with. Everything is a puzzle, is it not?

If you ask a businessman why he is troubled and unhappy, he will tell you 'what else'? He will tell you he has to take care of three businesses at a time. Whether a person has one, two or three businesses, at the time of death the only thing that will accompany him will be four coconuts and dried up ones at that too! 'I have to take care of three shops at a time. One is in Bhuleshwar, one in Fort and in this third shop here we sell cloth'. But even with three shops, if you look at his face, it appears as if he just drank some castor oil. He is preoccupied with his shops even when he is dining. Even in his sleep he is measuring the bales of cloth material. That will be his balance sheet at the time of his death. So beware!

How much thought should you give to your business? You should think about your business as long as your thoughts remain manageable. The moment they start to get out of control and make you worry you should stop. Otherwise they will destroy you and take you to your doom; in your next life you will find yourself with four legs and a tail! Do you understand?

[3] The Right Understanding Of Business

The purpose of being born in India as a human is for the attainment of liberation. Our lives are meant solely for this purpose. If you maintain only this as your goal, then whatever you achieve is fine. At least you should have a goal! The food you get is for this purpose. Do you understand? Is your life meant only for making money? Every living being is in search of happiness. Your life is for the knowledge of how you can attain liberation from all unhappiness. In this process you need to search out the path of liberation. Everything here is only for the purpose of attaining liberation.

People live for two reasons. Only a rare person lives for the Soul. All the rest live for money. The whole world has become obsessed with money and yet people find no happiness in it! Their bungalows remain empty the whole daylong and they are at their factories. They have all the material comforts but no time to enjoy them. One needs to acquire Atma Gnan. How long is one to wander blindly?

If someone were to ask what religion he should practice in his business, I would tell him that he should follow these three principles:

1) Ethical practice! The flow of money may increase or decrease. Never become unethical.

2) Maintain an obliging nature. If you do not have any money, at least ask people if you can be of any help to them. You can run errands for them instead. This is called an obliging nature.

Do not even harbor a desire of expecting something in return for what you do for others. The whole world has expectations in return for services they render; whether you wish it or not, you will be rewarded. There is always a reaction to any action. Your desires are nothing but actually begging on your part. They go to waste.

Questioner : What should one do to make progress towards the soul?

Dadashri : One should maintain his exclusive foundation of honesty. This faith is such that when he finds himself in a difficult situation, the inner energy and power will express. When he is not in a bind, and there is plenty of money around, there is no scope of the manifestation of these inner energies of the soul. Honesty is the only way. It will not happen with devotional worship of the Lord. If a person does a lot of bhakti but does not have honesty as his deep inner intent, there is no meaning in what he does. He must have honesty in his devotion. With such a base a human will become a human again. He will re-incarnate again into a human form. Those who cheat and deceive others, covet other people's wealth and wives are all doomed to take a birth in the animal kingdom. No one can change this. Their behavior here naturally binds their birth there. In the animal kingdom, there is no such thing as having one wife. Every female belongs to all other animals. Here married men are not supposed to look at other women lustfully, but this has become a habit with them and so they will be able to fulfill their desires when they go there into the animal kingdom. He will take this enjoyment for one or two lives there and then will straighten up and return to human life. The entry into the animal kingdom molds him so that he becomes fit for human birth again. After entering the human life he needs to mold further until he is ready for liberation. There is no liberation for those who are crooked!

There is no problem if you earn money honestly and ethically. You are hurting only yourself if you bring money by dishonest means. When you die that money will be left behind because nature will confiscate it. Moreover, in your next life you will still have to suffer the inevitable consequences of your actions.

Even if a man does not worship God, as long as he is ethical, it is enough. What is the point of worshipping God but living a dishonest life? It is meaningless. Even so we cannot make such a statement because people may stop worshipping God altogether and indulge in increasing dishonesty. The rewards are good if one is honest and ethical.

In this world happiness is to be found where there is complete ethical adherence. There is happiness for the one who maintains absolute ethics in his every worldly interaction. Happiness is also to be found in a person who lives for others and serves others. But this happiness is worldly in nature; it is temporary and illusionary.

Display the following statements prominently in your shop:

1)   Enjoy the present - do not worry about what is not in front of you.

2)   The Fault is of the sufferer

3)   Dishonesty is the best foolishness.

There is nothing lacking in this world. In this world there is everything. Is there not a saying:

'Sakal padartha hay jagmahi,
bhaagyaheen nar pavat nahi'

'In this world there is everything
He who has not the fortune will acquire it not'

Therefore whatever you can imagine, you can find in this world but you will only find these things if you have not created obstacles against them.

You need to have an unflinching honesty. God is not free to lend a hand. He is not free to give help to anyone. If your intentions are sincere and honest then they will indeed prove fruitful.

People claim : 'God helps those who are true', but it is

not so. If God helps those who are true, then what becomes of those who are untrue? Is God prone to partiality then? Surely God must maintain impartiality at all times? God does not really help anyone; in fact God would not meddle in this way. Happiness is experienced upon merely remembering God. What is the reason behind this? It is because God is the main thing within and that is your real nature and that is why you feel happy upon simply taking His name. You reap the benefit of His bliss. Otherwise God does not do anything. He never gives nor takes. And besides, he has nothing to give anyway.

Questioner : But how must we conduct business in our daily lives?

Dadashri : You must never let any inner turmoil (kashaya) come forth. Settle all dealings with equanimity. If you go to collect money owed to you and the manager of that business tells you to pay him ten thousand rupees in return for your check of five hundred thousand rupees, then settle the matter with equanimity. Now how much of a profit margin is there in your honest business? Also out of the five hundred thousand they owe you, only two hundred thousand is your personal money, the rest belongs to other people. It is also wrong if these people have to keep going back and forth for their money. So you should tell the manager that if you paid him ten thousand rupees, you would not be left with much profit. Try to make him understand and if he does not agree to accept five thousand, you may even have to settle with him for ten thousand for your money. Here you cannot say ' I will never succumb to bribery. Who does this man think he is?' If you maintain this attitude, who will answer to the people whose money is also tied up in this? Otherwise those people will curse you. Understand all this; act according to whatever the time and situation dictates.

It is not a crime to pay a bribe. But it is a crime if you do not know how to adjust to the worldly situation and crisis that presents to you. A lot of people will remain very stubborn in such matter and not give in. And you may hold on to your ethical principles as long as you do not antagonize anyone and you have enough money in the bank to cover everything. But what if you stand to lose the money in the bank and others come making their claims? What would you do then?

Questioner : Yes, you are right.

Dadashree: In my business I would instruct my clerks to pay bribes. Even though I conducted my business honestly and had no intention of stealing, I would tell my workers to pay the bribes. Giving someone the run around for his or her money is not right. So go ahead and pay the bribe if you have to. I do not consider bribes a crime but it is a crime not to pay your client in a timely manner, who has provided you with raw materials.

If you encounter a robber on your way, would you give him the money when he asks for it or would you refuse it as a matter of principle?

Questioner : I would have to give him the money.

Dadashree: Why do you give the money in that situation and not in this? These others are all robbers of the second kind. Don't you think so?

These are civilized robbers and those others are uncivilized. You may not have seen these civilized robbers. You may not have even come in the clutches of one but I have come across many.

Questioner : You are now on the spiritual path but at the same time you are still engaged in your large business, how are the two possible?

Dadashri : This is a good question. How can one eat flour and smile at the same time? You say that I claim to do business on the one hand and on the other I am walking on a spiritual path. How are the two possible? It is possible. Everything that takes place on the outside runs independently and everything that goes on within is independent also. Both are separate.

This Chandubhai sitting here is separate and the Soul within is separate. It is possible for the two to remain separate. Both the entities have different properties. When we have a mixture of gold and copper, we are able to separate the two, are we not?

Questioner : Yes we are.

Dadashri : In the same manner the Gnani Purush is able to separate the two. The Gnani can do whatever he wishes. If you want to separate the two and reap the benefits, then feel free to come here.

And the business will continue. But my attention is not engaged in my business for even a second. That business only carries my name. I have to tend to my business once or twice in a month for a few hours. And I do go there, but my attention is not focused there. What do you understand by focused attention? If you go to someone asking for a donation for a school, although he may not be inclined to do so, outwardly he may say yes to you for the donation. In the same way my mind is not in the business. Is it not so?

Questioner : Yes.

Dadashri : In the same way, everything here remains separate. There are ways to keep everything separate. The Soul is separate and so are the body and the mind..

I have not kept my chit in my business during my entire life. I have done business and worked for it but I have never had my chit in it.

Questioner : I worry about my business. I encounter lots of difficulties.

Dadashri : As soon as the worries start, you should understand that your work would be ruined. The work will not be ruined if the worries are not present. Worries are obstructive to work. A business can be destroyed because of worries. It is the nature of business to increase and decrease. Anything that increases will eventually decrease. No one can stop this process.

This process of filling does not affect our true wealth, the Self. The Self does not increase or decrease. That is how pure the worldly dealings are. This purity is because of this separation. Are not your children and wife partners in your business?

Questioner : They are my partners in my happiness and sorrow.

Dadashri : You are their guardian so why should the guardian alone do the worrying? Besides they tell you not to worry about them.

Questioner : What is the nature of worries? Worries were not there when we were born, so where did they come from?

Dadashri : As a person's intellect increases, so will his internal suffering. Was the intellect there when you were born?

In business it is necessary for you to think but if you go beyond thinking, then it will ruin everything. For that matter, even for your business you are free to think for ten or fifteen minutes but if things go beyond this time, things become complicated and you go beyond normality. Let go at this time. Thoughts about your business are inevitable, but when you become one with those thoughts, those thoughts will linger and will divert your attention and that is when you will have worries. This will cause a great loss.

Questioner : What should I do if I decide that I do not want to engage in artadhyana or raudradhyana, but if my shop is going into a loss and I have no choice but to do so?

Dadashri : It is the business that is running at a loss, not you. That is the nature of business; it will give you a profit and then a loss. It happens. One follows the other. The business will continue to show profit and loss.

Let me tell you what I used to do in my business? When steamers were launched, there were all kinds of puja rituals. We would even call a priest and do a puja of the ship and then I would whisper in the steamer's ear, 'You may sink if you want to, but that is not my wish. That is not my wish. That is not my wish.' If I did not say this, it would have meant that I was not interested and then it would sink for sure. By saying 'It is not my wish', the words would give effect and if the ship were to sink, then I would know that at least I did speak to it.

So in this world you have to make adjustments everywhere, in order to accomplish anything. The nature of the mind is such that if it does not get what it wants, it becomes depressed. That is why we have to resort to different tactics. Then if that steamer were to sinks after a few months, I would make an adjustment that at least it lasted six months. Business means sink or swim. Palaces of expectations are like a house of cards. They will bring disappointment. It is very difficult to remain unattached - vitarag in the worldly life. It is because I have the skill of knowledge and the skill of intellect that I am able to remain vitarag.

Once I incurred a loss in our business. This was before I attained Self-realization. At that time I was so anxiety-ridden that I could not sleep at night. The answer to my problems eventually came from within. I asked myself who else besides me was worrying about this loss? I felt that I was probably the only one doing so. My partner may not have been worrying at all; I must be the only one. The wives and children were also partners but they were unaware of this loss. Despite the fact that they were unaware of the loss, their lives were still going on. I was the only senseless one worrying about it! When I realized this I came to my senses. The worrying stopped.

Why are you stuck in the same corner as everyone else? You should walk in the opposite direction from everyone else. People will ask for profit, you should say 'Let there be a loss'; the one who looks for a loss will never have to worry. The ones who are looking for a profit will always have worries but not the ones looking for a loss. This I guarantee you.

When people set up a business they look for profit. They will say we are guaranteed a profit of twenty-four thousand in this project. Now when they forecast these figures, they do not take into account changes in circumstances. They never deduct the losses from such events.

I have been a contractor all my life and have been involved in all kinds of contracts. Amongst such contracts, we have even built jetties in the sea. Let me tell you what I used to do in beginning. Wherever there was a scope of making a profit of five hundred thousand rupees, I used to say to myself that it would enough even if we made a profit of one hundred thousand rupees. In the end even if we had enough to pay taxes and the daily expenses and broke even, that would be adequate profit. The profit would be of around three hundred thousand. This would keep the mind satisfied and content because we made way more profit than was expected. Here people expect a profit of forty thousand and get only twenty. Surely they are bound to be unhappy!

All businesses have two sons, one's name is profit and the other's name is loss. No one likes the son named loss, but nevertheless both will be there. They will always be born. If your business is experiencing a loss, does that happen during the day or night?

Questioner : It can occur both at night and during the day.

Dadashri : But shouldn't a loss only occur during the day? If a loss also occurs at night, how can it occur while we are asleep? This proves that it is really not under our control, otherwise why would the loss occur at night and for that matter how can you make a profit at night? Do you not incur a loss even when you work hard?

You may put in a lot of hard work in business or looking for a job and you keep your eye on everything from all directions and still if you get nothing in return, you have to understand that your circumstances are not favorable. Now in such circumstances, if you were to push yourself a little harder, you will incur even a greater loss. Instead you should concentrate on doing something for your soul. It is because you have neglected to do so in your past life that you are facing such difficulties in this life. It is a different matter if you have already attained Self-realization, but even the people who do not have this Gnan eventually leave everything up to God, do they not? What do they do? 'Whatever God does is correct', they say. And if a person were to assess the situation and look for answers through his intellect, he is bound to get nowhere.

People set out to make a living when their circumstances are not favorable. They should instead engage in bhakti (worship) during such times. You should do bhakti, work towards the salvation of your soul, stay in satsang etc. It does not matter if you cannot afford to buy vegetables; at least you have enough grains for a meal. You will earn only if your circumstances are right otherwise people make a loss in a lucrative business and a profit in an unproductive one. It all depends on your circumstances.

Profit or loss, neither is under your control. Just go along with all these natural adjustments. What happens if you make a profit of one million and immediately loose half a million? As such people cannot even tolerate a loss of one hundred thousand. They cry and worry and some even go mad! I have seen many such people who have gone mad.

Questioner : In order to attract customers, I open my shop early and close it late, is this correct?

Dadashri : Who are you to attract the customers? You should open your shop at the same time other shopkeepers do. And it is also wrong for you to open your shop at nine-thirty when other shopkeepers open theirs at seven thirty. Close your shop when others close theirs. What does the worldly law dictate? It says you should observe what others do. Go to sleep when others do. What nonsense if you make a racket at two in the morning when everyone is asleep? This is like worrying about how you are going to digest your food, after you finish eating! You get the result of that in the morning don't you? It is the same with business also.

Its like this: if a person's chit does not wander to his factory when he is having his meal, then his factory is fine, but if his chit wanders there, then of what use is that factory? Such factories will make you have a heart attack. So you have to understand what is normal. If a person has to manage three work shifts and he is newly married, what will happen if he does not have time to see his bride? Are those three work shifts appropriate? He has brought home a new bride; surely he has to keep her mind at peace. When he goes home his wife will complain that she never sees him and that he does not even have time to talk with her. So this is not fair or proper, is it? Everything should be fair and proper in this world.

You must agree and concede to issues related to the family business in order to avoid clashes at home with other family members. Say, 'yes, yes'. Let what is running keep running smoothly, do not obstruct it. But everyone should collectively come to a decision: for example decide on a final amount say one and a half million rupees, beyond which no one wants any more. Everyone in the family should be present in this decision making process.

Questioner : No one will agree in such matters Dada.

Dadashri : Then it is of no use. Everyone one must agree.

You may even run four work shifts. If you do, will it grant you an extension to live two hundred years more?

Questioner : How much should we expand our business?

Dadashri : You can expand your business to the point where you can sleep soundly. You may even expand to the point where you are able to remove it from your mind when you want to sleep. You should not invite trouble, which is unnecessary.

Is there not a relationship with the shopkeeper and the customer? Does that relationship end when the shopkeeper closes his shop? No it does not. The customer will remember how the shopkeeper treated him. He will remember if the shop-keeper sold him bad merchandise. People will always remem-ber and bind revenge, so even if you close your business in this life, they will not leave you alone in your next life. They will not rest until they have avenged themselves. This is the law of hurt and revenge. That is why the Lord has said to become free from vengeance by any means that you can.

Once an acquaintance of mine borrowed some money from me. He never came back to return the money he bor-rowed. I understood then that this was because of some un-settled account from past life. I told him that he did not have to return the money and that he was free to keep it. If you are able to break the recurring cycle of vengeance by letting go of your money, do so. Break the vengeance by whatever way you can otherwise even one person's vengeance will lead to your wan-dering life after life.

Even if hundreds of thousands of rupees were at stake, I would let it be. Because that money is bound to go and I am bound to remain. Whatever the situation, I will not let any kashay take place. What remains to be said even if you loose a hun-dred thousand rupees? At least I am still here and the rest is dispensable.

I separate everything – if the business was running in a loss, I would say, 'The business has suffered a loss'. We are not the owner of profit and loss so why should we take on the burden of profit and loss? Profit or loss does not touch us. If for some reason there is a loss in the business and the income tax has to be paid, I would tell the business, 'Business, if you have anything to pay the taxes off with, do so. You are the one who has to fulfill this'.

If someone were to ask me, 'Have you incurred a loss this year?' I would say 'No, I have not had a loss, the business has'. And if there was a profit I would say, 'The business made the profit.' I do not have profit or loss.

Questioner : Certain things do not bother us much but sometimes when we expect to make a profit in our sales and end up making a loss, it keeps gnawing at us.

Dadashri : You should deposit such losses the moment they occur in your 'account of losses' and by making an entry of this in your books as a loan paid off, you can clear your accounts. You have many opinions ahead of time that you will make a certain amount of profit but you end up making a loss so you have to tell yourself that it is all vyavasthit. If you are to incur additional loss, it will happen if it is in your vyavasthit. So these profits and losses are not in your control. You will incur a profit even if you say you do not want it. You may say you are tired of all the profits and that you do not want any profits any more but even then you will not be able to stop it. Even when you say no, there will be a pressure of both profit and losses. So do not keep an account of your profits and losses.

If some businessman pressures me and insists that I visit Calcutta by plane despite my objection, what would I do? He remains absolutely adamant. For such situations you cannot keep accounts. You have to go and spend the money for the airfare and other items. Never keep accounts for money that comes and goes. On the day you incur some loss, deposit that money into your account of losses and offset it with the positive income in the virtual trust account. It does not exist but it is there within your mind. You still have a balance on the books. These books are not permanent. Do people not destroy these books after a few years? Would they destroy them if they were real? These are all solutions to keep your mind at peace. The day you incur a loss of one hundred and fifty rupees deduct if from the earnings of five hundred that you have in the virtual account, so you will be left with the sum of three hundred fifty. Therefore instead of seeing a negative figure (loss) of one hundred fifty, you see a positive figure of three hundred fifty. This is how the world is – The world is not precise, it is approximate. A principle would be precise and exact. But this world is capricious whereas the account of liberation is an absolute and exact principle.

What do you call equanimity? Equanimity means that the profit is the same as the loss. Equanimity is to remain unaffected when you realize a loss instead of a profit, and also a profit where you expected profit. It is where you do not become elevated or depressed. It is to rise above the duality.

If people asked me how my business was doing, I would tell them whether it was making a loss or even a profit. Generally I would not discuss my business. If someone asks me whether my business was making a loss, I would tell him if it were true. My partner has never questioned me why I tell everyone about the business. It would be better to tell the truth because it would prevent people extending loans to us, and this would help reduce our liability. On the contrary people tell me 'Why do you say it out in the open? They will not lend you any money'. But that would only increase our debts instead. Why not say it as it is?

If your business made a loss, tell this openly to the other person. The other person will say a prayer on your behalf and it will make you feel better by discussing it with someone. If you keep it to yourself, the burden will be too heavy to bear.

Whatever worries you are faced with, just take them in your stride. Before Gnan I used to have a lot of worries when I was doing business. Only under such circumstances will such a Gnan manifest. I handed out sweets to everyone even when my children died.

When I experienced sudden difficulties in the business, I never used to discuss them. When Hiraba found out she would ask me how much of a loss we had incurred. I would tell her we did not incur any loss. In fact I would offer her some money and tell her that it was the money the business had made. And when Hiraba would insist that people were saying the business was running at a loss, I would insist that it was not so and that in fact we had more income but that she was to keep this a secret.

When my business experienced a loss, it affected so many people that they would come to me asking how much we had lost. I would tell them that we did have a loss but now all of a sudden we just made a profit of one hundred thousand ru-pees! This would pacify the other person.

I would analyze all experiences. I never worried about money in the business. There is no one more foolish than the one who worries about money in his business. Money is already written in your destiny. Do losses not incur even when you do not worry about them?

If you have dishonest employees who are stealing money from your business, you should understand that your money is not honest money and that is why you have encountered such people. How would you otherwise come across such dishonest people? I too had experienced this situation once when all I came across were people who were crooked. That is when I decided that I did not want any part of this.

A good business is one that does not involve any violence or aggression against other living entities. Some grain vendors mix their good quality grain with an inferior quality. When a person resorts to such practices, he will regress into an animal life form in his next life. One must do business honestly otherwise dishonesty will creep in.

In your business you will make a profit of $66,616 whether you do business honestly or dishonestly. So then how do you want to conduct your business?

You just have to make an effort in your business and scientific circumstantial evidences (vyavasthit) will automatically organize everything. However, you still have to make the effort and not become lazy. God has said that everything is vyavasthit. Whether you make a thousand or a hundred thousand, your cunningness and deceit will not increase your profit by a single penny. On the contrary your cheating will bind new accounts for next life.

Questioner : If the person we are dealing with is being cunning, should we not do the same in return? That is what people do nowadays!

Dadashri : This is precisely how the disease of cunningness sets in. But the person who has the knowledge of vyavasthit, he will remain absolutely calm. If a person is being cunning when he deals with you, quietly find your way out the back door, but do not resort to the same cunning ways.

What I am trying to say is that do you have to worry whether you will have water to bathe or a mattress to sleep on? In the same way money will be there for you without your giving it much thought.

There is no need for you to keep an inner intent (bhavana) to earn money. Let your efforts continue, however. What happens when you have inner intents? If I grab the money for myself, there will be none left for the other person. Let whatever quotas have been assigned to people naturally, be. So then what is the use in keeping an inner intent? That is what I am trying to say. Doing this will prevent many people binding demerit karma. That is what I am saying.

There is tremendous essence in this single sentence, but only if you understand it. It is not mandatory that people take this Gnan of mine. If a person has not taken this Gnan but understands that everything is very precisely allocated and nothing occurs outside of one's account, it is enough. Would you not otherwise understand if you experience a loss even when you are working very hard? Because hard work is hard work, you ought to be rewarded for it, but do you not also experience a loss even when you work hard? The account of life after life is very precise and exact.

The only objection is in your entertaining an inner intent towards money, nothing else. I do not have any objection towards any of your other actions. People will read this but they are not able to understand. They will read everything here but the essence within this sentence is very profound.

As long as you are not familiar with the wrong and the dishonest, the wrong and the dishonest will enter your business.

Questioner : But even when we know what is right in the business, we are not able to say so.

Dadashri : That shows that the worldly dealings are not under our control, but our inner intent is. To plant a seed is in our control, to reap the harvest is not. If you do something wrong, your internal intent should be, 'this should not be so'.

A true boss never has to utter a word. If a boss scolds, we have to assume that he is an assistant and not the owner of the company. A true boss would never have a frown on his face. He would create an agency that would take care of the scolding but he would never reprimand. Such a boss would help both the disputing parties to arrive at a compromise. He would concede that both the parties are correct from their perspectives; he would bring about a resolution in this manner.

There was a big economic slump in 1930. During this time of scarcity, wealthy businessmen 'sucked' the 'blood' of their workers and now during times of prosperity, the workers are sucking the master's blood. Such is the rule of this world. During times of depression, the master preys on the workers and during times of prosperity, the workers prey on the master. Both will take turn against each other. That is why when these masters complain about the workers, I tell them that in 1930, they did not spare any of the workers and that is why these workers will not spare them. If you do not make it a practice of preying on your workers, you will not encounter anyone who will prey on you. Even in this time of kaliyug, you will not encounter anyone who will do you wrong.

Even within your own home if you try to dominate and

oppress your wife when the times are good, she will do the same when the times are bad. So always keep your days of feast and famine the same. If you live with honor and dignity, everything will run smooth for you.

This world has never been without justice, even for a moment. Only justice prevails from one moment to another. This world is not able to tolerate injustice, even for a moment. Whatever injustice is taking place is justice itself in action.

Questioner : I have incurred a tremendous loss in my business. What should I do? Should I close the business and start another? I have a lot of debts.

Dadashri : Losses incurred in a cotton trade cannot be recouped in a grocery trade. Losses incurred in a business can only be recouped from the same business and not through employment. Would you be able to recover losses of contract business from a beetle nut shop? Wounds can only heal in the trade in which they were incurred, the remedy only lies in the same trade.

You have to maintain only the intent that you do not want to hurt anyone in the slightest degree. You should keep your inner intent pure that you want to clear all your debts. Money is the eleventh life energy, therefore do not retain anyone else's money. There is no problem if someone else has your money, but your goal should only be that you want to pay back every dime. First keep this goal in your awareness

Questioner : What is the reason behind a person's intentions becoming bad?

Dadashri : When bad things are to happen in his future, he will be compelled from within: 'Go ahead and do what you want, don't worry about the consequences'. This happens because his fate is destined to turn bad. Coming events cast their shadows beforehand.

Questioner : But is he able to prevent or stop it?

Dadashri : Yes, he is able to stop it. If he has acquired Gnan, then he will be guided from within to repent his ill thoughts. He will be guided to maintain an inner intent of 'things should not be this way'. In this manner, he is able to stop it. His ill thoughts come because of his past knowledge, but today's knowledge tells him that this is not the right thing to do. Then he is able to turn things around. Do you understand? Are things becoming clearer?

It is not just for hundreds of thousands of rupees that people spoil their inner intent; alas they spoil it even for twenty-five rupees! The problem is not with him wanting to enjoy himself, but it is with the knowledge he has acquired which tells him: 'Why do you want to give it away? Why not keep it and enjoy it for yourself? We will worry about the rest later on'. This is the wrong knowledge that he has acquired.

That is why I tell anyone that comes here that he or she can engage in whatever business they want to, but they must keep a pure inner intent of wanting to pay off all their debts. Besides who does not like money? Tell me this, who does not like money? Everyone likes money. Therefore you should never have an inner intent that the other person losses his money. Keep the intent of: I want to pay off my debt, no matter what happens. Keep such a decision from the very start. This is the most important thing. If you become insolvent in other matters, it is fine, but you should not become insolvent where money is concerned, because money causes suffering. Money is called the eleventh life energy so you can never deprive anyone of his or her money. This is the main point.

Questioner : What happens if a person dies leaving behind a debt?

Dadashri : A person may die leaving behind a debt, but from within he must have purity of intent till the very end: 'I want to return the money. Not only in this life, but also in the next life, I must repay the money.' If a person maintains such intent, then he will not have any problems. There are many who will ask, 'Why do you want to take and give? Who is going to question you up there?' Then his case will be that.

Still the principle is that he can borrow money only if he has the intention of paying it back. After that he should resolve every four days that he wants to return that money as soon as possible. If you have such an intention then you will be able to repay the money, otherwise God only knows!

If you have borrowed money from someone and if your inner intent remains pure, then know that you will be able to return that money and you don't have to worry about it. All you have to be aware of is whether or not your inner intent remains pure. You can also tell from the intent of the person who has borrowed from you. If his intent does not remain pure, then you should know that you are going to lose that money.

Your inner intent must be pure. Your inner intent means what you are able to do as your own right. Pure intent is 'If I had all the money I owe, I would repay it today'. In your intent you should maintain only that you want to return the money as soon as possible.

Questioner : If a person is not able to fulfill his debt and files for bankruptcy, will he have to repay his debt in his next life?

Dadashri : He will not be able to see money again. Money will not even touch his hand! Our laws state that you should not spoil your intent when it comes to returning money you have borrowed. Then only money will return your way again and you will be able to fulfill your debts. No matter how much money you have, ultimately it will not come with you so get your spiritual work done. You will not encounter the path to liberation again. The path of liberation will not return for another eighty-one thousand years. This is the final 'stand'; there is nothing ahead.

The debt is not about money in this world. It is the debt of previous life's attachment and abhorrence. If it was money that was the real debt, then would I not tell you, 'Pay off the debt in full otherwise you will not be set free'. Instead I tell you to settle your debts with people, with equanimity; settle all matters with equanimity, even if it means that you have to pay the other person in order to do so. Having done so, ask the other person if he is happy with the settlement, and if he says he is, then the matter has been settled with equanimity.

Wherever you have committed attachment and abhorrence, these attachments and abhorrence will meet you again. You will have to settle these accounts by all means and suffering. This whole life is meant for settling all your accounts. Everything from birth to death in this life is mandatory.

A creditor kept harassing one man. That man who was being harassed came to me and told me that the collector would shout a lot of abuse at him. I told the man that he should call me the next time the collector called on him. The man sent his

young son to call me when the collector came to his house. I
went to his house and sat outside listening to the collector. He
was calling the man all kinds of names. I then entered the home
and asked the collector if he was the collector and he replied
that he was. I told him that he and the other man had a contract
between them; the man was going to return the money and he
was going to accept it, but the abuse he was hurling at the man
was not part of the contract. It was an extra item. This extra
item had a price. I told him that he would be charged forty
rupees for every abusive sentence he uttered. The contract did
not include the provision for abuse, and he was breaking the
contract. When we say it like this, they will be sure to behave
and not become abusive. I say things with such intensity that the
other person will stop swearing and cursing and straighten up.
This is for his benefit.

If a person does not return the two hundred and fifty
dollars you had given him, and that money is gone, whose fault
is it? The fault is yours. The fault is of the sufferer! You will be
able to practice true religion through this knowledge, and you
will stop blaming others, and your kashayas (anger, pride, attachment and greed) will come to an end. That is why the
sentence 'Fault is of the sufferer', is capable of liberating you
completely. This sentence has come forth exactly.

Questioner : Before this Gnan manifested within you,
you must have been prepared and ready.

Dadashri : Nothing of the sort! I did not know anything
and that is why I failed my metric examination. One thing I did
notice was that my strength of character was very high but even
then I committed dishonest acts. I used to go with other boys
to eat berries, which grew in people's farms. Is that not stealing

when you take the mangos and fruits from other people's trees?
When I was young I used to go with other boys to eat mangos.
I too used to eat the mangos, but I would not take any home
with me. All I know is that my character was noble.

From the time I started doing business, I do not recall
that I have ever thought about my self and the business. For me
the business ran on it's own. But if you were to come to me,
I would inquire after your business, I would ask whether you
have any problems in your business. I would help you with your
problems. If some other person were to come to me, I would
ask him the same. So I was always involved in other people's
problems. This is what I had done all my life. I have not done
any business at all, except I do know how to do everything. If
a person were having problems and getting confused with no
solution even after several months, I would find a solution for
him within just one day.

I could not tolerate anyone's suffering. If someone had a
hard time finding a job, I would write letters of recommendation
to people I would not ordinarily speak to, but when it came to
helping people I would address them in my letters as 'Dear
elder brother'! One way or another I would find solutions to
help people.

When I was doing business, I had one understanding with
my partner. During the time that I was working, only that amount
of money that I would legitimately earn as a salary would be
sent home. Nothing more. Therefore that money would be pure
for sure. The rest of the money stayed in the business. My
partner asked me what we were to do with the retained money.
I told him that if ever the income tax office demanded a payment for something, he should take the money from the business

and make the payment, and not send any letters from the tax department to me.

Questioner : If someone owes us money and does not pay it back when he is supposed to, do we accept it as having fulfilled our past life debt and be content with the situation?

Dadashri : Not like that. If that person is rich and honorable then you should pursue the matter but if he is poor then don't make the effort to collect.

Questioner : Should I make the effort to collect or just sit at home and assume that if he is going to return the money, he will do so on his own accord and if he does not then do I assume that my past debt has been cleared?

Dadashri : No, no don't assume so much. You have to make the necessary efforts. You can tell him: 'At the moment I am a little short of cash, if you have the money, can you please make arrangements to send it to me?' Speak to him with respect and discretion and if the money does not come then understand that you have settled some past account with him. But if you don't even make the effort, he will take you for a fool and he will go on the wrong track.

Everything in this world is a puzzle and in this puzzle man gets so much beating life after life and is beaten to death after death. He has taken this beating for countless lives but when the time comes for him to escape this cycle, he does not take the opportunity. Then the opportunity does not come again. Only a liberated person can liberate others; what can a person who is bound, do for you? Only the liberated one is worthy. The moment the thought occurs to you: 'What's going to happen if he does not return my money?' your mind will start to become weaker. The element of suspicion is introduced. Once you lend money, just decide that you have folded all that money in a bundle of black cloth and thrown it in the ocean. What hopes do you have of retrieving something once you throw it in the ocean? Give without any expectations of any kind otherwise do not give.

In this world there will always be interactions of give and take. So, if you lend money to people, sometimes some will not return the money, but you cannot be preoccupied and agitated over whether the money will be returned or not. If you do so, where will it end?

I was in a similar situation once, but I never worried about whether that money would be returned. I did however remind that person from time to time that he owed me some money. A man had borrowed five hundred rupees from me. There was neither a record nor a promissory note for this transaction. I had forgotten all about it until I encountered that man a year and half later. I asked him if he could return the money and he asked me, "What money?" I said, "The money that you borrowed from me." He said, "When did you loan me the money? On the contrary, I am the one who loaned you the money and you are the one who has forgotten". I immediately understood the situation. I told him that I did remember and asked him to come home the next day to collect it. I gave him the money the next day. This incident actually happened to me. What can one do if such a man were to come pestering for money?

How is anyone to deal with a world like this? If you were to bundle up some money in a black cloth and throw it in the sea, is it not foolish to think that you will get it back? If a person returns the money to you, you should invite him for tea and thank him for his graciousness in returning the money. You can say to him that it is indeed a wonder that he is returning the money because in this age of Kaliyug money does not come back. The fact that he is returning what he owed is more than enough; do you understand? This is what the world is like. There is suffering in returning the money and suffering in taking it back. Who can be happy in this? What is more, it is all vyavasthit. It is vyavasthit when a person does not return the money and it is also vyavasthit when you lose double the amount.

Questioner : Why did you pay that man another five hundred rupees?

Dadashri : I did not want to have another situation with that person again in my future life. The awareness I had when he demanded the money he owed me, was that I was on the wrong track.

During the years 1942 to 1944, when I had enough money, many people borrowed money from me. Then in 1945 at the age of 37, I decided that I wanted to pursue the path of liberation. I decided that I would not collect on the money that was owed to me, because if people were to pay me back part of what they owed, they may return for some more and my dealings with them would never come to an end. If I tried to collect the five thousand that was owed to me, that person would come to borrow ten thousand. Instead I would be better to leave the five thousand with him. He in turn might think it would better if I never bumped into him. If he saw me in the street, he would cross over to the other side, so I understood. I wanted to be free from all these people, and these people in turn set me free.

What is natural law? What has happened is justice. Do not look for justice. If you look for justice, you will have to hire an attorney and go to court. Instead accept whatever happens as justice. If you want to be liberated, you will have to accept this principle and if you want to wander life after life, then you should seek justice through the courts of law. When you begin to accept natural justice, you will become free and if you seek justice in a court of law, you become bound.

You go thrice to collect your money and the person who owes you is not to be found. Then when you finally meet him, he frowns and mistreats you. This path is such that you will not have to chase anyone to collect your money and on the contrary he will come to your home to return it. When after making several attempts to collect your money, you are finally promised that you will have your money by the end of the month, at that time if there is no reaction on your part (your internal state is in equanimity), then that money will come to your home. But you have reactions, do you not? Does your internal state not change? From within you feel: 'This person is senseless, he is a worthless, he makes me run around' Do you not feel this way? So when you go back to him, he curses you. It is because of changes in your internal state that the other person treats you in this manner.

Questioner : Does that mean that we are making the other person behave badly?

Dadashri : We have spoilt everything of our self. We ourselves have created whatever obstacles we face. The other person is not responsible at all. So how can we rectify this? No matter how much suffering the person you are dealing with subjects you to, you should not have a single negative thought about him. This is the solution for making him come around. By doing this, everything becomes better for you and for the other person. The people of this world will have negative thoughts. That is why I am telling you to deal with every situation in life with equanimity. By equanimity it means that you should not have any negative thoughts about the other person.

When you are trying to collect from your debtor and he is not able to pay you because he has no money, then you should not be persistent. He will bind vengeance against you and should he take birth as a ghost in the celestial world, he will harass you to no end. How is the poor man at fault when he is not giving you the money because he has none? Do others have the money but refuse to give?

Questioner : What should we do if he does not return the money even when he has it?

Dadashri : What can you do even then? The most you can do is file a claim in the court. If you beat him up, the police will arrest you.

It is best if you do not take the matter to the courts. A wise man will not do so, his premise would be: 'If the money is mine, it will come to me otherwise it will not', but he would not invite such demons unnecessarily. Otherwise these demons will harass you for no reason. Some people call their debtors all kinds of names even before their case goes to trial. They will say: 'You imbecile, you have no sense.' To these people I ask, 'and you have a lot of sense?' This is a person you are referring to, not a donkey. How can you speak in this manner?

Say a person borrows money from you but does not pay you back and you are unable to collect it legally because of statute of limitations. Now that person may escape the legal consequences of the worldly law, but he will not escape the consequences of the nature's law. As far as the law of nature is concerned, people are made to pay back the sum with interest. A person may not have any recourse under the worldly law

but under nature's law he will be paid back with interest. Therefore if someone is not paying you back the three hundred rupees he borrowed from you, you should at least make the
attempt to collect it. Why should you do this? Because if this
person is not paying you back even the three hundred, just think
about the interest nature will assess on this amount. And in a
matter of one hundred to two hundred years, how large will this
amount become? Therefore you should try to collect the money
from him so that he would not be subject to such severe consequences. But if he insists on not paying you and puts himself
in this predicament, then you are not responsible for it.

Questioner : What is nature's interest rate?

Dadashri : The natural interest is one percent per year.
It is one rupee for every one hundred. One rupee! If he does
not pay you back your three hundred rupees, it is fine. You
should not have any hard feelings. Just maintain a cordial relationship with him; even play cards with him because you are not
going to lose anything. Nature is so precise and exact that even
if someone has stolen a single strand of hair from you, it will
come back. Nature is absolutely correct, all the way down to
the sub-atomic particles. So there is no need for you to retain
a lawyer. Neither should you be afraid of being robbed. People
read about incidents in the newspaper about day light robbery
where a woman is pulled out from her car and robbed of all the
gold she was wearing, or someone was beaten and the robbers
ran off with all his money. People start to worry whether they
should wear their gold jewelry. Do not worry. Even if you go
around wearing precious gems worth millions of rupees, no one
will touch you, if it is not in your account. This world is like that,
and it is correct. You will be affected only if you are karmic
liability. That is why I am telling you that you have no superior

over you. Therefore don't worry, become fearless.

In your business, do not take anything that is not yours and on the day you end up doing so, there will be no substance in your business. God does not meddle in this. In your business the only two things that will help you are your skills and your honesty and ethics. If you are unethical, you will prosper for a year or two but after that you will incur a loss. If you happen to do something wrong, you will still become free of any liability as long as you repent for your actions. Ethics is the essence of worldly dealings. If you are ethical but do not have a lot of money, you will still have peace of mind and if you are unethical but have a lot of money, you will be miserable. Religion without honesty and ethics is no religion. Ethics is the foundation of religion.

It is like this. Be completely ethical if you are able to be so. If not, then at least make a decision to be ethical at least three times a day. The fourth time you may let go and be unethical. It is still ethical to be unethical as long as you set a limit. Maintain honesty in your dishonesty. As a representative of the vitarag Lords, I am telling you that as long as you as keep your dishonesty in control, in the bounds of disciplined limits, you are ethical. This discipline will take you to moksha. I am not concerned whether you are honest or dishonest, but keep a discipline and limit over what you do. The whole world has pounded everyone in their worldly interaction with the guilt of 'thou shall not' and I am the only one who is saying, 'go ahead, do not worry, be unethical, but do set a limit and stick to the discipline. You will not be responsible from then on'. Of course the ideal thing is to remain honest and ethical.

I am saying that be unethical if you cannot avoid it but do it within limits. Resolve that you want to be unethical to a certain degree and no more. I will take ten rupees unethically every day in my business. If any more than this sum, say five hundred comes my way, I will not touch it.

This sentence of mine is very profound. If a person were to understand this, his work is done! God too will be happy with him: He wants to graze in someone else's pasture, but he does so within limits! Otherwise where is the limit when people start grazing in some one else's pasture?

Do you understand this rule? Practice the principle of limits in dishonesty, do you? What I am saying is, 'If you are short of money all the time but you do not want to accept bribes, how long can you go on fighting the matter? Furthermore, you invite more problems when you borrow money from friends.' So I tell him that he can resort to being dishonest, but within limits. A person who exercises limits in his dishonesty is better than one who is completely honest, because the honest man has an ego about his honesty, whereas this person will not have this disease.

No one would teach you such a thing! To practice dishonesty within limits is a great feat.

The person who sets limits to dishonesty will achieve liberation, but how will the one who never takes bribes or is never dishonest achieve liberation? It is because the latter is intoxicated with the ego of his ethical behavior. God too would dismiss him with the smugness he wears on his face. I am not telling you to accept bribes but I am saying that if you are going to be dishonest, then set a limit when you do so. Set yourself a limit that you will only take five hundred rupees in bribes and no more. Even if a person offers five thousand rupees, you will not accept it. If you are running short of say five hundred rupees to run your household every month, then take only this amount in bribes. Only I take on such a liability by telling you to do this because in this day and age what are poor people to do if they do not take bribes? Cooking oil, ghee and sugar is so expensive nowadays. These people have to pay their children's school fees! Just look at the price of a can of cooking oil, are they not quoting seventeen rupees for it?

Questioner : Yes.

Dadashri : So it is acceptable when a businessman does illegal hoarding and black marketing, but no one will speak up for the servant! That is why I am saying that you can be dishonest but do so within limits. That limit will take you to moksha. Bribes do not obstruct you; it is the lack of limit, it is greed that obstructs.

Questioner : Surely it is wrong to be dishonest?

Dadashri : Generally it is considered wrong but the Lord has a different definition. In the eyes of the Lord the objection is not against honesty or dishonesty but against the ego. Honest people have tremendous ego. They are intoxicated even without drinking alcohol!

Questioner : Now if a limit of five hundred rupees has been set for bribes, is a person free to take more if his needs arise because of inflation or emergencies?

Dadashri : No, once a limit has been set one has to follow it. Five hundred means five hundred and he has to stay within that limit.

How is man to cope with all the difficulties of the present time? And on top of that where is he to get the money he falls short of? He finds himself in a bind because he has nowhere to turn. This way the money comes to him and if he takes the bribe, his problem is solved altogether. Otherwise a man can go on the wrong path altogether and he will continue to take increasing bribes. It is better that he takes this middle path where he will be a little dishonest but he will still maintain honesty. His daily living becomes easy and he will be able to run his household.

If you understand what I am saying from the simple basic perspective, then salvation will be yours. If you understand each of these sentences, then liberation is yours. But what happens if you interpret it according to your own intellect? Everyone has his or her own language and intellect based viewpoint, which prevents him or her from understanding this, 'discipline in dishonesty'.

I too am a businessman. I too have to contend with running a household and pay income tax. I do a business, which involves contracting work, and such business by nature is corrupt and yet I remain detached. How am I able to remain detached? Because of Gnan and people are suffering because of ignorance.

Questioner : I do not wish to do anything dishonest, but I am forced to.

Dadashri : You must repent for doing anything, which you have no control over. You should sit quietly for about half and hour and repent your actions. Since you have disclosed your feelings of remorse, you are not liable. Pratikraman should be done for your actions you are made to carry out against your wishes. If you become of the opinion that what you do is correct, then you will be liable. There are people who take pleasure from their wrong deeds. You feel repentant because you have a lighter load of negative karmas. In that sense, you are closer to liberation. Others do not even feel any remorse.

If you have a lot of money, there is nothing better than donating it to a temple of Simandhar Swami or other vitarag Lords (Omniscient Lords). And if you do not have a lot of money, then the best thing is to feed mahatmas, people who have acquired Self-realization through this Akram path. If you have little less, then give to someone in misery, but do not give cash. Send them food, clothing etc! So if you want to make a donation, you can do so even with little money.

[4] THE STATE OF DETACHMENT

No one shares in the liability incurred in conducting business dishonestly. These 'bags of intellect', the egoistic businessman, will keep indulging in misdeeds. The father tells his children he is stealing in order to make money for them and the children tell him he can do so if he wants but they do not want money earned from such dealings. Even his wife tells him that all his life he has been dishonest and that he should now stop, but does he listen? No he will not.

From the moment man learns to give, his intellect will turn positive and good. He has not learnt to give in countless previous lives. He does not like to let go of that which has been used and is now simply refuse, such is the nature of a human being. He has a habit of only accumulating and hoarding. Even when he was an animal, he was taking but never giving. He turns towards the path of liberation from the time he learns to give.

The moment he receives a check he thinks to himself: 'I will get the money as soon as I deposit this check.' The check he receives was predestined; these are benefits of past good deeds he is reaping today. What effort did he make in reaping these benefits? People will say 'I earned the money because I worked so hard'. I say you only deposited a check. Where is the effort in it? Besides you only get the amount on the check, do you get any more from it?

I am telling you to delve over this with great seriousness. Calm down. What the whole world is doing in running after this money is a natural event of filling and emptying, plus and minus according to the law of karma. They are complicating it, multiplying and dividing through their kashaya in running after it. These people are spoiling their next life. And absolutely no difference will occur in their bank balance. Everything is natural, so how are they going to oppose nature? I alleviate your fears by assuring you that nothing is in your control. I am disclosing to you everything as it is. No one has any authority of manipulating one's credits and debits. Any increase or decrease in money in the banks is in the hands of nature. Otherwise the banker would keep only one account; he would have only credits and no debits.

Do not get into arguments with anyone. You will encounter such people on rare occasions. What will you achieve by arguing? And if one happens to get into an argument with you, you can tell him, 'At least have the fear of God', and if he tells you 'What God? What nonsense?' then you will know that he is a potential for trouble.

There is no greater sin than becoming helpless and without initiative. Should this helplessness be even allowed? People become helpless and depressed if they don't have a job, they even become so when they incur a loss, they become feeble and helpless when an income tax officer scolds them. What is he going to do? The most he can do is take away your money and your home? Is he going to be able to take anything else?

Why must you become weak and helpless? To be this way is a gross insult to God. If you become helpless and weak, it insults the God within you. But what can God do?

What is the law of worldly monetary transactions? Do not try to make up for your losses incurred in the stock market through a grocery business. Try to recoup your losses through the stock market only.

Whether there are two mosquitoes or a lot in the room they will not let you sleep. So you should say: 'listen here o world of mosquitoes! Even when just two mosquitoes do not let me fall asleep, then why don't you all come as well?' Profit or loss is nothing but mosquitoes. Mosquitoes just keep on coming. You just have to wave them away and go to sleep.

Within you, lies infinite energy. The one with infinite energies will ask you, 'So Chandubhai, what do you think?' The intellect within will respond, 'There has been such a big loss in this business. What will happen now? Try to recover that loss by taking up another job'. The one with infinite energy will say, 'Chandubhai why don't you ask me, why are you asking for advice from the intellect? Ask me, I have infinite energy'. People seek profit from the very entity (intellect) that makes them incur a loss. You incur a loss from a different entity (karma effect) and are seeking the solution to it from another entity (the intellect). How will you be able to recoup from your losses in this way? You are the abode of infinite energy. If you don't spoil your inner intent, then there is no power in this world that will go against your wishes. Such is the nature of the infinite energy within you. The inner intent must be that you do not want to hurt anyone to the slightest extent through your thoughts, speech and acts. The laws of your inner resolve must be so strong that you will not go against that law even if it means loss of your body. You can lose your body only once, so there is no need to be afraid.

If people become anxious and scared so easily, then no one would engage in any business transactions. I have seen many prominent men who talk about making a demand on promissory notes in excess of hundreds of thousands of rupees. These are brokers themselves. They come to me. They are fearful and worried about what people are saying about them. They worry about what is to become of them. I encourage them and tell them to be patient and strong. I tell them that even when they drive around in cars, which travel, at high speeds, they are able to reach home safely every time, so why would they not come out safely from their business? When we travel in cars if we feel that we will get into an accident, will we be able to travel? People do not go around banging into other cars do they? They are able to safely maneuver in an out. The same happens in business. If you were to succumb to fear so easily when you go out, then you would not even step outside the house to come from Santacruz to Dadar. The fact that you have arrived here is because you are not afraid; you are not afraid because of your unawareness of the possibility of an accident. So you should be strong. So you must recover from the very place where you incurred the loss. Do not change your location or business. I know that this is the correct way from the perspective of the relative laws.

You should oblige others with whatever you are capable of. Whatever you do, give happiness to others. Every morning make a decision that you want to give happiness to whomever you meet. There are many other ways of helping besides giving monetary help; you can help a person who is in a dilemma by talking to him, making him understand and giving him encouragement. You can even give a little money if need be.

Whatever responsibility you take for helping others, you are actually doing for yourself.

Questioner : To do for others is to do for yourself, how does that work?

Dadashri : Every Soul has the same quality. So whatever you do for the soul of others, reaches your own soul. Whatever you do for the comfort of others will also benefit you. Whatever you do for the soul will open the path of liberation for you. And whatever you do for their worldly comforts, will give you happiness here and now. This is the only difference.

Questioner : My uncle has trapped me in this business. Whenever I think of it, I feel intense anger and inner turmoil towards him and I keep questioning why he did this to me. What should I do? I find no solution.

Dadashri : Your uncle is doing this to you because of your own mistake (from past life). When that mistake is over, no one will be able to trap you. As long as you come across people who trap you, the fault lies with you. You are not done with all your faults. Why do I not come across anyone who will trap me? I cannot find anyone to trap me even though I am looking for someone to do so and if someone tries to trap you, you try to escape. I don't even know how to escape. How long will people try to trap you? People will trap you as long as you have some pending karmic account; as long as you have some account left to give and take. All my accounts are closed now.

Some time back I went even as far as to tell people that if they have a need, they should come to me for money, but they should slap me before they take the money. People told me if they were a little tight for money they would somehow manage but what would become of them if they were to slap me? Now,

I cannot say this to any ordinary Joe Bloggs; I can only say this to people with spiritual development.

So there is no one in this world that can trap you. You are the owner of this world and no one is your superior. Only God is your superior. But once you have the realization of your God, the real Self, then no one is your superior. No one can touch you. But alas, look at how people have become trapped!

So get rid of this notion in your mind that your uncle has trapped you. But if people ask you, you do not have to say that it is because of your own mistake that your uncle has trapped you, because people do not have the awareness and the understanding of this Science. You must communicate with them, in their language. You can tell them 'My uncle did this to me', but from within you must understand that he has done so because of your own mistake and that whatever Dada has told you is correct. Furthermore this is a fact, because your uncle is not the one suffering at the moment, he is enjoying himself with a fancy car. His mistake will become evident when nature catches up with him but today it is you that nature is holding accountable.

If you do not go to your shop, your shop will be unhappy with you. If your shop becomes happy, you will be able to make some profit. In the same manner, you should come and spend some time in this satsang. If you can't stay long it is fine. Stay just for five or ten minutes, if I am here. Your presence has to be noted.

This check of Dada is a blank check. It is not something you have to use freely. Use it when you find yourself in a major bind. You can pull the emergency chain if there is an emergency but if you pull it just because you dropped a packet of cigarettes, you will be fined. So you must not misuse it.

Questioner : These days the taxes are so high, that large businesses cannot offset the expense without cheating. When everyone ask for bribes a person has to cheat, does he not?

Dadashri : You may cheat but do you feel any remorse from within? When you feel remorse and are repentant, it will lighten your liability.

Questioner : But what should we do in such circumstances?

Dadashri : You have to understand that it is wrong to cheat and you must repent sincerely when you do. You only become free if you feel uneasy within about what you have done. In this day and age you have no choice but sell goods you purchased in a black market, in a black market. So you should tell 'Chandubhai' to do pratikraman. Before you did not do pratikraman and that is why you have filled these 'ponds' of karma. Now you can clean it all up by doing pratikraman. Who is the doer of this greed? Chandubhai is the doer. If you sell your goods in the black market, you must tell Chandubhai: "Chandubhai, there is no objection in your selling in the black market. It is under the control of vyavasthit. But you must do pratikraman and vow not to do it again'.

If someone tells me: 'I do not want any religion, I want worldly happiness'. I would tell him to practice honesty and ethics. I would not tell him to go to the temples. Giving to others is the religion of a celestial being. Not taking what belong to others is the religion of man. Therefore honesty is the highest religion of all. Dishonesty is the best foolishness. But if I cannot be honest, does that mean I have to jump into a lake? My Dada has taught me to do pratikraman every time I am dishonest. Your next life will be beautiful. Know dishonesty as dishonesty and repent for it. Without doubt, the one who repents is an honest person.

There is a solution for having made money dishonestly. If the day has passed in making money dishonestly, at night tell Chandubhai, 'Why were you dishonest? Now repent, four or five hundred times. Do pratikraman now'. The Self is flawless and does not have to repent. But Chandubhai has to do this. Make him repent.

When you have a disagreement with your partner, you immediately become aware that you have already said more than you should have. So you should immediately do pratikraman for it. Your pratikraman should be instant, like cash payment. This bank is a cash bank and so is the pratikraman that is being done instantly.

Let me explain to you how obstacles in life are created. If you tell your assistant that he has no sense, then you will have created a barrier on your own sense. Now just look at this! People in this entire world have wasted away their human life by becoming trapped in such obstacles and barriers. You have absolutely no right to call other people senseless. When you make such a statement, the other person will respond with an inappropriate statement also, and he too will create an obstacle for himself. You are responsible for creating this barrier for him. So tell me how is the world to be saved from such obstacles? If you call someone useless, it will create a barrier on your own worthiness. But if you immediately do pratikraman for saying this, the obstacles will be destroyed before they are created.

Questioner : In order to fulfill my responsibilities at work, I have insulted many workers by speaking very harshly with them. I have treated them very badly.

Dadashri : You must do pratikraman for all that. You did not have bad intentions in doing so. You were not doing it for yourself; you did that for the government. And that is considered your sincerity.

[5] GREED PERPETUATES WORLDLY LIFE AFTER LIFE

Greed is to become perpetually engrossed in anything that becomes dear to you. Greed is the reason why you find no satisfaction even after you acquire it. A greedy person is preoccupied with his greed from the moment he wakes up until he goes to bed at night. That is called greed. From the moment he wakes up he is driven by his greed; he does not even stop to relax. He does not have the time to laugh. He is consumed with his greed the whole daylong. The moment he enters the market, his greed is there. Greed, greed, greed and greed. He roams around in this way the whole day long, in vain. When he goes to the market, he knows exactly where the vegetables are expensive and where to find cheap ones. He then heads for the stall that sells cheaper vegetables every time.

A greedy person accumulates everything for the future. When he collects a lot, a couple of large rats will come in and clean up everything he has hoarded.

You are free to save and accumulate money, but without a desire to accumulate it. Do not obstruct money if it comes your way and do not go digging for it if it does not.

Money is destined to come to you. It will not stay just because you want it to stay. It will leave when it is time for it to leave. You cannot obstruct or accumulate it. If you save up enough today in the hope that it will be used for your daughter's marriage twenty-five years later, you are mistaken. If people believe in this, they are wrong. Whatever comes your way at that time is the reality. Money must be fresh.

So use everything that comes your way, do not waste it. Do not throw it away. Use it for a good cause. Do not have a strong desire for accumulating it. There should be one principle about accumulating money and that is that there should be a limit to how much you accumulate. That is called the necessary capital. Retain the capital and spend the rest in the right places. You cannot waste money.

Contentment is the opposite of greed. This contentment comes from an inner understanding carried over from the past life. This understanding is different from Gnan, which is Self-knowledge. This understanding which is the knowledge of the relative world, results in his being content and not running after money. Without this understanding greed remains.

One has enjoyed all this in many previous lives, and therefore there is contentment that he does not want anything. The one who has not enjoyed these things in his past life is discontent. There remains within him a constant need and greed to enjoy this, enjoy that etc. Then greed of many variety sets in.

Questioner : A greedy person is also miserly is he not?

Dadashri : No, misers are different. Misers do not have money and that is why they are misers. A greedy person may have twenty five thousand rupees at home, and yet he is constantly looking for cheap bargains. His chit is always in greed. Even when he goes to the vegetable market, he is looking for the cheaper pile!

The greedy person has awareness about everything in the worldly matters.

Questioner : What is the difference between a greedy person and a miser?

Dadashri : A miser is only concerned with money whereas a greedy person has greed about everything. He has greed for money and greed for pride. Greedy people have greed spread out in every direction and will take away everything for themselves.

Questioner : Which is better, to be greedy or thrifty?

Dadashri : Greed is a crime. Thrift is not.

What does it mean to practice economy? When times are tight, be tight and when times are relaxed, you should relax also. Never get into a debt over anything. You can create a debt in your business, but not for your enjoyment or any luxuries. When is it acceptable for you to get into a debt for food? Only when you are dying, and not otherwise it is unacceptable. You cannot get into a debt to enjoy fancy and gourmet foods.

Questioner : Dada, is there a difference between miserliness and thriftiness?

Dadashri : Yes, a tremendous difference. If you earn a thousand rupees a month, then you should keep an expense account of eight hundred rupees. And if your income is five hundred rupees then you should have an expense account of four hundred rupees. That is called thriftiness. A miser, however will spend four hundred rupees only, whether his income is a thousand or two thousands rupees. He would not use a taxi. Thriftiness is economics. It helps maintain awareness of future financial difficulties. People despise a miser the moment they see him, whereas people do not feel that way about a thrifty man.

How should you practice frugality in your home? Practice

it in such a way that it does not appear bad to others. Frugality should never enter your kitchen. You should practice generous frugality. If frugality were to enter into your kitchen, then your mind will become ruined when you have guests and you have to feed them. If a person were very extravagant, I would tell him to practice noble frugality.

You do not have to have an ongoing inner intent for earning money. Let your efforts continue. What happens when you keep having a desire for money? If I pull the money towards me, other people fall short in their allocated quota. This means that I am snatching away their quota and there will be nothing left for them. So accept whatever quota has been allocated to you naturally. The meaning of greed is to take away what belongs to others. What need is there for you to have and harbor an ongoing intent to earn and accumulate money? Do you have a desire to die? Death is inevitable and so is money that is going to come to you as your share. People will stop committing sins with just this one sentence of mine.

The conduct that results from greed is what leads a human into an animal life form.

You are a good person and if you do not allow yourself to be conned, then who will? Greedy and unworthy people can never be conned. They will con everyone. The noble person is the one who knowingly allows himself to be cheated. The one who welcomes you with profuse greetings is in fact making a pre payment to you before cheating you.

That is why it has been written about the Gnani as one who will allow himself to be cheated by the greedy. This is because my sole desire is moksha. I have not come here to accumulate wealth. And I also know the ultimate reason for a person being cheated and for a person to cheat someone. I know about this, and therefore it does not matter.

I have not been conned because of my naivety. I am fully aware when people are cheating me. I deliberately allow them to do so. Foolish are those who get cheated because of their naivety. Do you think that I am naïve? Those who deliberately allow themselves to be cheated, would you call them naive?

My business partner Kantibhai once told me that people took advantage of my naive nature. I told him that because he is calling me naive means that he himself is naive. I deliberately allow other people to cheat me. He then told me that he would never make such a comment again.

I understand what the other person's intentions are like, I am aware of what his intellect is like so I let the poor fellow go. I have come here in order to become free form all kashayas. I allow myself to be cheated in order to prevent kashayas and that is why I let them do it again and again. Is there not fun in deliberately allowing yourself to be cheated? There are not many people who knowingly allow themselves to be cheated.

From a young age, I had maintained the principle of deliberately allowing people to cheat me. It is not possible, whatsoever, for people to make a fool of me and take advantage of me.

What happens when you knowingly allow people to cheat you? Your brain becomes very powerful. Not even the top judges have such a brain.

Shrimad Rajchandra has said that one should serve a Gnani with his mind, body and wealth. Someone asked him what use would a Gnani have for wealth; a Gnani has no need for anything in this world. The answer to this is that giving money where the Gnani directs makes one free from the Gordian knot of greed. Otherwise the greedy person's chit hovers around money life after life.

A man once asked me to get rid of his greed. He said that he had a big tuber of greed within him. I told him greed is not something that you can get rid of. I told him his greed would break naturally when he incurs a big loss. Then he will say he wants nothing to do with money! The tuber of greed will be destroyed through incurring a major loss.

This knot of greed will loosen when a loss is incurred. When a person incurs a big loss, his greed will vanish in a hurry. All other tubers, inner junk of negativity will vanish, but not the one of greed. There are two gurus for a greedy person: a trickster and a loss. If a greedy person incurs a loss, the loss will demolish his tuber of greed very quickly. The other guru for the greedy is the swindler and the con artist. They will promise the moon to a greedy person who becomes easily tempted and before you know it, all his money is gone.

People ask me when they will be able to experience the bliss of the Self in all its glory. I tell them a person can only experience this bliss when he becomes free from all desires. All tubers of greed have to go. The one who has a tuber of greed experiences no happiness whatsoever. So give away everything, whatever you give is yours.

Happy are those who spend whatever money comes their way. Those who spend their money on the right path will be happy. That money will build up a credit in their karmic account. Otherwise it is bound to go into the gutter. Where is it headed? It is all headed into the gutters. Where does all the money in the city of Bombay go? Into the gutters, vast amounts are going into the gutter. Money spent towards a good cause will come with you but not any other kind.

Money will not remain where there is contempt and gossip. When people are contemptuous or engaged in bad mouthing others, wealth will not come their way.

When will this country of ours become wealthy? When will it become happy and prosperous? This will happen when both contempt and slander are put to rest. If these two stop, the land will prosper with boundless new money and wealth.

[6] SUBTLE UNDERSTANDING OF GREED

Questioner : There are certain faults that last for many lives; they bind a person to take birth over and over again. Which faults are these?

Dadashri : Greed! Greed stays with a person for many lives. A greedy person becomes greedy in every life because he likes greed.

Questioner : A person has millions of rupees and yet he is unable to give towards good causes, what is the reason for this?

Dadashri : How can one become free from the bondage he has created? No one can become free. He remains bound. He cannot even eat and enjoy himself. For whom does he hoard his money? In his past life he lingered around his buried wealth as a snake, guarding it: 'My wealth, my wealth.'

Only the person who shares his wealth with others knows how to live life. Whatever he gets he gives freely to others! That is called living life. You must not squander away your wealth in madness. Spend it wisely. Madness is squandering it on alcohol and other addictions. Nothing positive comes out of this. Give freely; just like this man here, does he not give freely? That is the result of the highest kind of merit karma. It will result in binding of the highest kind of merit karma.

Dadashri : What is merit karma of the highest order? It is when a person gives happiness to others without any expectations of anything in return.

Questioner : How can we take money to the next life with us?

Dadashri : There is only one way. When you give happiness and peace to those who are not related to you, it will come with you. The only benefit you get by giving peace and happiness to those related to you is that you will be clearing your karmic account with them, but you will not reap rewards that will go with you to your next life. Another solution is that if you were to ask someone like me, then I would tell you to give money that will facilitate the spread of the knowledge of the Self, so that others may benefit. You can give towards printing of books, which will impart this knowledge so that those who read these books will be guided towards the right path. I will give the suggestion if people ask me, but otherwise I do not have any personal interest in this.

A person may believe: If I collect and save up this much money, it will give me happiness and I will never be unhappy again. But in the process of collecting it and keeping it safe, his greed is perpetuated. He becomes greedy himself. You are to practice frugality, you are to practice economy and spend money wisely, but you are not to practice greed.

How does greed enter and take hold from within? Where does this process start? Greed is not present in a person when he has no money. But when he gets ninety-nine rupees, greed enters when he wants to turn his savings into an even hundred by adding a rupee. He thinks that he will not spend anything towards the household today and add one more rupee to this balance. This is called the 'shove of ninety-nine'! When a person gets this shove his greed will not be contained even when his hundred rupees turn into five million. This greed only breaks when a Gnani jolts him!

From the moment he wakes up, a greedy person keeps practicing his greed; his entire day is spent consumed in greed. The vegetables are too expensive, he will say. His greed manifests even when he needs a hair cut; its only been twenty-one days since my last hair cut, it will not matter if I wait till the month is over. Do you understand? His tuber of greed keeps showing him such cues for saving money and he thus keeps perpetuating his kashayas. Of all the inner enemies, greed and deceit are very difficult to get rid of.

A greedy person will not spend whatever little change he has in his pocket. He will not spend to travel in a rickshaw even though he has difficulty walking. I told such a person not to do this. I told him to start spending ten rupees at a time for rickshaw rides. He told me that he is not able to spend that way; he cannot even enjoy his meals in peace when he has to part with his money. He told me that he knew feeling this way was very wrong but what could he do, he was helpless. His prakruti, his nature was holding him back, so I told him that he should take some loose change with him and drop a little at a time on the road as he is walking along. He did this one-day and then he stopped.

If a person were to do this a few times over, his mind would realize that it no longer has any control and the person does not listen to it anymore. So it would stop; in this way the mind and everything else will turn around. You have to act contrary to the mind; you have to shake it up a little. If people in your household get out of control, you have to shake them up a little, in the same way if your mind gets out of control; you have to shake it a little.

What do we mean by a tuber of greed? A person has a constant awareness of how much and where his money is. So much is in the bank, so much is with such and such person, so much is held up in this project – this remains constant in his awareness. He will never have the awareness of 'I am pure Soul'. His awareness and preoccupation with money must be broken; his awareness must be engaged in his real Self.

The intrinsic characteristic of a greedy person is that he will not be influenced by anything. He cannot be 'colored' (influenced) by anything, he remains unaffected by anything. He remains 'yellow', whether you dip him in red color or green color. If a person is greedy, all you need to understand is that he will not be colored by anything.

Those without greed will be easily colored. When the greedy person laughs, everyone will think he is colored and is in with the rest of the crowd. Not so. The greedy person will listen to everything I say, he will even say that this Gnan is very good and that he feels very happy just listening to it but from within nothing touches him. Others forget all about their worldly life and possessions in this satsang but not the greedy one. He will not forget his greed; he is thinking if I leave now and if that other person also leaves, I will go with him in his car so I can save five rupees. Other people forget everything; they don't even think about saving money in fares. They become entranced in the satsang but the greedy one will not forget anything; that is called not being colored. Do you understand? Have you not heard people say 'I am completely colored in the colors of Dada'? The greedy person will never be colored with Dada, no matter how much you dip him in colors.

A person may feel like donating some money but it is the tuber of greed that will not let him do so.

Questioner : Sometimes the circumstances are such that a person wants to give and yet he is not able to.

Dadashri : That is a different matter altogether. In those situations you have the awareness of the circumstances. But it is not like that. You will be able to give once you make the decision to do so.

Questioner : Yes but despite having the money, one does not give.

Dadashri : A person will not be able to give even if he has the money. He is simply not able to. His greed will not allow him to give. If his greed breaks then he will be liberated. It is not that easy.

Questioner : But every one has the ability to give a certain amount!

Dadashri : No, it is not so, because of greed. A person with greed may have a million but he will find it extremely difficult to part with even four pennies. He will become ill. And when he reads in the scriptures that one should serve a Gnani Purush with one's body, mind and wealth, he develops a fever by thinking, 'Why do they write such things?'

There are two definite ways to break greed. One is when

a Gnani Purush breaks it through the power of his speech. And the other is when a greedy person incurs a heavy loss; at that time he will say that 'I am not going to do anything anymore. I will make do with what I have.' I have to tell so many people that their greed will break when a loss comes their way and not otherwise. It will not break even by what I say. Such is the intensity of this tuber.

Heavy losses have broken the tuber of greed in people. A better way is through the instructions, Agnas of the Gnani. But who can improve and help the one who is not ready to abide by a Gnani's instructions?

The tuber of greed will dissolve only if one remains in this satsang, because unless one comes into satsang, he will not even be aware of his greed. If a person stays in the environment of satsang, he can see purity taking hold in the relative self, Chandulal. In satsang this happens because the Self remains separate. We can observe everything unperturbed, and that is why we are able to see all our faults. By not being in the satsang we become the tuber and it is impossible to see any faults. That is why Krupadudev has said: 'If I cannot see my own faults, then what other solution is there?'

Our lives should be spent for the benefit of others. Just as this candle. Does it burn for it's own light? Does it not burn for others? Does it not burn for the benefit of others? In the same way if people were to live for the benefit of others, there is an automatic gain for them in it. Death is inevitable regardless of whether you do for others or not, so why not do for others, because you will inevitably benefit from doing so. If you make others miserable, your misery is in it for sure. You can do whatever you want to.

Whatever you do to know and attain your real Self is the main production and because of this main production, the by-production will automatically be there and whatever you need for your worldly life, will come to you. I only keep one kind of production: 'May the entire world attain permanent peace and many attain liberation'. This is my main production and because of this I continue to get the resultant by-production. The tea and snacks I get served are different from what you get served. Why is that? It is because my production is of a higher quality. In the same way if your production were of a higher quality, your by-production would also be of a higher quality.

All we have to do now is just change our goal, nothing else. We have to decide on our goal and keep that goal in mind, nothing else. Money should not remain in our awareness.

Questioner : What is the right use of money?

Dadashri : When you use it for others or for the Lord.

Questioner : What should we do if money does not last?

Dadashri : Money is something that will not last. But change the way it is used. If it is flowing in the wrong path, change the path so that it flows on the path of religion. How ever much of your money flows on the right path that much is true money. Money will last only after God arrives in your home, how else will it remain?

If your money flows on the wrong path, then put a control over it. If it is flowing on the right path, then decontrol it.

A man is giving some money to a poor person and another person with a lot of intellect tells him: 'Wait! Why are you giving money to this man?' The man gives the money anyway and the poor person takes it, but just by making the comment, the intellectual person created an obstacle for himself whereby when he is unhappy and needy, he will not find anyone to help him.

[7] THE FLOW OF CHARITY

From now on you can erase everything through repentance and you should make a decision not to make comments like, 'Money should not be given to others in charity'. If you inadvertently happen to do so, then you should ask for forgiveness and it will be erased. This is like changing the contents of a letter before you mail it. Once the letter is mailed, it is too late, so change the contents before it is too late. Before you had commented that it was wrong to give money in charity and now you are erasing that comment by saying it is good to give to charity, so your previous belief gets erased.

Only your religion and spirituality will help you at the time of need, so let your money flow in the path of religion.

What is the nature of money? It is restless and mobile. It will come but one day it will go away. So spend your money for the good of others. Whenever you are faced with bad circumstances the only thing that will help you is what you have given to others. So you must have this understanding ahead of time. Surely money should be spent on the right path?

There are four kinds of charities: They are food, medicine, knowledge, and freedom from fear.

For charity of knowledge, you may print books that will guide people on a good path and bring salvation for them. When you give such knowledge, you will reincarnate in a higher life form or you may even go to moksha, attain liberation.

The Lord has placed emphasis on the charity of knowledge, and where no money is required He has talked about abhayadaan, freedom from all fear. Where there is a transaction of money, He has talked about charity of knowledge and where a person does not have a lot of money; He has talked about charity of food and medicine.

The fourth is abhayadaan; this is where your conduct will not cause any living being to feel any fear.

Questioner : In this day and age, a person will give illicit money towards the path of religion. Will he bind any merit karma?

Dadashri : Of course he will! Did he not part with that much money? Did he not sacrifice that much money? But it is his intent behind doing so that will dictate his merit karma. The fact that he gave the money is not the only thing that is taken into consideration; the fact that he sacrificed the money is indisputable. The plus and minus are determined by where the money came from, what was his intention behind giving and then whatever is left over, is his. His intention is that instead of the government taking it away, why not give towards this cause?

Questioner : Is it not considered violence (himsa) to hoard money?

Dadashri : Of course it is violence. To hoard is to commit violence because that money cannot help others – can it?

Questioner : In the scriptures to give with some expectations in return is not recognized as a charitable act. The scriptures also do not look down upon this intent of charity.

Dadashri : It is best if you do not keep any expectations. To keep expectations renders the karma groundless and without any essence of purity. What I am saying is that even if you give five rupees, give without any expectations.

If there is a man who donates one hundred thousand rupees to charity and wants his donation commemorated with a plaque and another man who gives one rupee but he gives anonymously, then the donation of the latter is of much greater value. The amount of donation is irrelevant. By having plaques displayed, people zero out their 'balance sheet'; whatever they give in donation, they exchange with a reward of a plaque and recognition. The one who donated even one rupee keeps his balance because he gives anonymously.

Questioner : What should I do if a lot of money comes my way, more than my needs, due to my merit karma?

Dadashri : Then spend it. Do not keep much for your children. You can spend the money to educate them, to teach them and once everything is done and they become employed, then you should not keep much money. Keep some aside in the bank, some ten or twenty thousand which you can give to them should they come across some difficulty. But you should not tell them that you have set this money aside for them, otherwise they will encounter difficulty even when they are not supposed to.

A man once asked me: 'Should we not give anything to the children?' I told him that he should give to his children whatever his father gave to him. We should give it all to the children and the remaining difference is ours and we should spend it on a charity of our preference.

Questioner : As a lawyer I can share this with you Dada. The law mandates that whatever property one inherits, he must pass it on to his children and whatever he makes on his own he is free to spend according to his will.

Dadashri : Yes he can do whatever he wants to. He must do it himself with his own hands. The path of liberation dictates that a person should keep his own wealth separate. If he were to spend it by giving to charity, he will carry forward the benefits of this act. Even after taking this Gnan, you still have one or two more lives to come and there you will need your merit karma. Even when we go out of town, we carry some food with us, so will we not need something for the next life?

Questioner : What should we do in this life in order to gain some merit karma for the next life?

Dadashri : Donate one fifth of your income in this life towards the temple of the Lord. Spend one fifth to make other people happy. This much 'overdraft' will definitely reach there. What you are enjoying in this life is the 'overdrafts' you created from your past life. The merit karma of this life will carry forward to your next. Your current earnings will be of benefit to you in the time ahead.

[8] MONEY AND RELIGION

On the path of liberation, there are two things that cannot exist: Thoughts about women and thoughts about money. There is no religion where there are thoughts about women or money. It is because of people's attachment for these two that this world continues to perpetuate. So a person is mistaken if he is looking for religion or spirituality where these two exist. Having said this, how many spiritual centers run without money today?

A third requirement for the path of liberation is : Right vision. Do not waste your time where there are dealings with money and women. Choose your guru carefully. If he has any impurity, any interest or need for money or woman, do not make him your guru.

The one for whom any neediness for any worldly thing is completely gone, is the one who is worthy of every spiritual sutras, gifts of this world. But first all traces of any beggary, desire or need in a person must go – only then! There are so many types of inner needs and desires: the need for money, the need for fame, the need for sex, the need for disciples, the need to build temples; every need of any kind is nothing but beggary. But how can anyone's needs, be quenched here?

In relation to these matters of worldly gurus, a man once asked me whether it is the customer or the vendor that is at fault. I told him, 'Of course it is the customer! The shop keeper can open up any business he wants to, but should the customer not be able to discriminate?'

A true spiritual teacher (sant purush) will not take any money. People seek a spiritual teacher because they are unhappy and suffering and top of that the teacher swindles them of their money! It is because of these kind of so called 'sant purush' that this country of India is in ruins. A true sant purush is the one who gives his happiness to others, not take happiness from others.

This association of Dada's workers is pure. I wear my own clothes; I wear my own dhoti. I have bought my clothes with the money that I myself have earned and that is why I go around looking a little scruffy. If the association were to buy my clothes, then today you can even buy dhotis for four hundred rupees can you not? Not only do I not accept anything from the association, but neither does Niruben. Niruben stays with me and takes care of me. She also wears her own clothes, which she buys herself.

Whatever purity you have, this world is yours by that much. You are the owner of this world by as much purity you have within you. I have not been the owner of this body for the past twenty-six years and that is why I have complete purity. So become pure. Pure!

Purity means that there is not a single worldly thing that one has a need for. Such a person is free of any beggary.

If you were to feel remorse even now, you will be able to destroy your sins. Meditate solely on your remorse and re-pentance. What should you repent for? Repent for the money you have cheated people out of. Remember each and everyone of them, recall their faces, recall your sins: wherever you have acted immorally or have been adulterous, wherever you have viewed others with lust, these sins can be destroyed if you try to wash them out even now.

When can you help others achieve salvation? It is when you yourself become pure – absolutely pure. Purity will attract the whole world. Anything pure will create attraction. Impurity fractures the world. So there is a need to acquire purity.

Jai Sat Chit Anand

Prayer to Pure Self

Oh pure Soul within me, You reside within all living beings, just as You reside in me. My real nature is the same as You. My real state is Shuddhatma, pure Soul. Oh Lord, pure Soul, with utmost devotion and oneness, I offer my salutations to You.

I confess to You all mistakes * that I have committed in my ignorant state. I am sincerely and deeply repentant for these mistakes and ask for forgiveness. Dear Lord, please forgive me, forgive me, forgive me, and grant me the energy never to repeat such mistakes.

Dear pure Soul, my Lord, please bless me with such grace that this feeling of separation from You terminates and that I attain oneness with You. May I remain merged in You and remain as one with You.

(* Recall the past mistakes that you have committed)

Pratikraman : Process of Divine Apology

With Dada Bhagwan as my witness, I offer my salutations to the Pure Soul who is totally separate from the mind, speech and body of * _____

I recall my mistakes (aalochana) **

I apologize for these mistakes (pratikraman)

I affirm not to repeat these mistakes again (Pratyakhyaan)

Dearest Dada Bhagwan ! Grant me the strength to act in accordance with this firm resolution.

* name of the person hurt by you.

** recall the mistakes you committed with this person.

Books of Akram Vignan of Dada Bhagwan

1. Adjust Everywhere
2. Ahimsa : Non-Violence
3. Anger
4. Aptavani - 1
5. Aptavani - 2
6. Aptavani - 4
7. Aptavani - 5
8. Aptavani - 6
9. Aptavani - 8
10. Aptavani - 9
11. Autobiography of Gnani Purush A.M.Patel
12. Avoid Clashes
13. Brahmacharya : Celibacy Attained With Understanding
14. Death : Before, During & After...
15. Flawless Vision
16. Generation Gap
17. Harmony In Marriage
18. Life Without Conflict
19. Money
20. Noble Use of Money
21. Pratikraman : The master key that resolves all conflicts
    (Abridge & Big Volume)
22. Pure Love
23. Right Understanding to Help Others
24. Science of Karma
25. Science of Speech
26. Shree Simandhar Swami : The Living God
27. The Essence Of All Religion
28. The Fault Is Of the Sufferer
29. The Guru and The Disciple
30. Tri Mantra : The mantra that removes all worldly obstacles
31. Whatever Happened is Justice
32. Who Am I ?
33. Worries

'Dadavani' Magazine is published Every month

Persons to Contact

Dada Bhagwan Parivar

Adalaj : **Trimandir**, Simandhar City,
Ahmedabad-Kalol Highway, Adalaj,
Dist.: Gandhinagar - 382421, Gujarat, India.
Tel : (079) 39830100, **Email :** info@dadabhagwan.org

Ahmedabad : **Dada Darshan**, 5, Mamtapark Society,
Behind Navgujarat College, Usmanpura,
Ahmedabad- 380 014. **Tel. :** (079) 27540408

Rajkot : **Trimandir**, Ahmedabad-Rajkot Highway, Nr. Targhadiya
Cross Road, Maliyasan Village, Rajkot. **Cell.:** 9274111393

Bhuj : **Trimandir**, Behind Hill Garden, Airport Road,
Near Sahyognagar, Bhuj (Kutch). **Tel. :** (02832) 290123

Godhra : **Trimandir**, Village-Bhamaiya, Opp. FCI Godown, Godhra,
Dist.-Panchmahal. **Tel. :** (02672) 262300

Morbi : **Trimandir**, Village-Jepur, Morbi-Navlakhi Road, Morbi,
Dist.-Rajkot. **Tel. :** (02822) 297097

Vadodara : **Dada Mandir**, 17, Mama ni Pol (Street),
Opp. Raopura Police Station, Salatvada, Vadodara.
Cell. : 9924343335

Mumbai : Dada Bhagwan Parivar, **Cell. :** 9323528901

Bangalore : Dada Bhagwan Parivar, **Cell. :** 9590979099

U.S.A. : **Dada Bhagwan Vignan Institute :**
100, SW Redbud Lane, Topeka, Kansas 66606
Tel. : +1 877-505-DADA (3232) ,
Email : info@us.dadabhagwan.org

U.K.: **Dada Darshan (UK)**, Unit 2, Columbus House,
Stonefield Way, Ruislip, HA4 0JA
Tel. :+44 330-111-DADA (3232),
Email : info@uk.dadabhagwan.org

Kenya : +254 722 722 063   **Singapore** : +65 81129229

Australia : +61 421127947   **New Zealand :** +64 21 0376434

UAE : +971 557316937   **Germany** : +49 700 32327474

www.dadabhagwan.org, www.dadashri.org

What Is the Gnan Vidhi?

It is a scientific spiritual process of gracing people with the experience of Self-realization. It is the gracing of real Knowledge that separates the Self from the non-Self or the worldly self. This session is different from the regular *satsangs* in the form of questions-answers sessions.

The Knowledge that manifested within Pujya Dadashri, also known as Dada Bhagwan in 1958, is the very same Knowledge that is graced upon all seekers through the medium of *Atmagnani* Param Pujya Deepakbhai, with the grace of Dada Bhagwan and the blessings of Pujya Niruma.

Why Should You Take Gnan – Knowledge of the Self?

1. To awaken and experience the Soul; your real Self.

2. Inner peace due to destruction of all wrong beliefs and the attainment of the right belief of 'I, the real Self am pure Soul'.

3. To attain liberation from the cycle of birth and death.

4. Demerit *karma* of infinite past lives are destroyed.

5. To experience eternal peace, happiness and harmony with all living beings.

6. To get solutions to carry out your worldly life through right understanding.

7. You finish paying off all past *karma* and you do not bind any new ones.

Is It Necessary for One to be Physically Present for the Gnan Vidhi?

1. *Gnan Vidhi* is the result of the *Gnani's* grace and blessings. It is necessary to attend this *Gnan Vidhi* in the direct presence of an *Atmagnani*.

2. Spiritual information acquired through watching *satsang* programs of Pujya Niruma and Pujya Deepakbhai on TV or VCD, books etc. can help you prepare the background for attaining *Gnan* but they cannot give you Self-realization.

3. Any instrument used for attaining *Gnan* can help you to attain peace but for awakening of the Soul, only the *Gnan* taken in the direct presence of an *Atmagnani* will give you the experience. For example if you want to light your candle, you need a real burning candle, a picture of a burning candle will not do.

- **You do not have to change your religion or your guru to attain this *Gnan*.**

- **You do not have to pay anything to attain this *Gnan*.**

Jai Sat Chit Anand

Books of Akram Vignan of Dada Bhagwan

1. Adjust Everywhere
2. Ahimsa : Non-Violence
3. Anger
4. Aptavani 1
5. Aptavani 2
6. Aptavani 4
7. Aptavani 5
8. Aptavani 6
9. Aptavani 9
10. Autobiography of Gnani Purush A.M.Patel
11. Avoid Clashes
12. Brahmacharya : Celibacy Attained With Understanding
13. Death : Before, During & After...
14. Flawless Vision
15. Generation Gap
16. Harmony In Marriage
17. Life Without Conflict
18. Money
19. Noble Use of Money
20. Pratikraman : The master key that resolves all conflicts (Abridge & Big Volume)
21. Pure Love
22. Right Understanding to Help Others
23. Science of Karma
24. Science of Speech
25. Shree Simandhar Swami : The Living God
26. The Essence Of All Religion
27. The Fault Is Of the Sufferer
28. The Guru and The Disciple
29. Tri Mantra : The mantra that removes all worldly obstacles
30. Whatever Happened is Justice
31. Who Am I ?
32. Worries

'Dadavani' Magazine Is Published Every Month

Contacts

Dada Bhagwan Parivar

Adalaj : **Trimandir**, Simandhar City,
Main centre   Ahmedabad-Kalol Highway, Adalaj,

         Dist.: Gandhinagar - 382421, Gujarat, India.

         Tel : +91 79 39830100, **Email :** info@dadabhagwan.org

Toll free inquiry number for USA & Canada
1-877-505-DADA (3232)

USA Email : info@us.dadabhagwan.org
Canada Email : info@ca.dadabhagwan.org

Ext.	Name of Activity/Center	Ext.	Name of Center
10	Gurupurnima Information	1019	Milwaukee Center
11	Satsang and Gnanvidhi	1007	Minneapolis Center
12	Books VCD and DVD	1025	Montreal Center
13	Dadavani Coordinators	1020	New Jersey Center
14	Kids Team	1021	New York Center
1011	Atlanta Center	1024	North California Center
1004	Birmingham Center	1022	Oregon Center
1012	Champaign Center	1002	Philadelphia Center
1027	Charlotte Center	1008	Phoenix Center
1005	Chicago Center	1003	Raleigh Center
1026	Dallas Center	1017	Simi Valley Center
1013	Houston Center	1015	Tampa Center
1009	Los Angeles Center	1006	Toronto Center
1016	Lowell Center	1010	Virginia Center
1018	Maryland Center	1023	Wilmington Center

Australia : +61 421127947

Germany : +49 700 32327474

Kenya : +254 722 722 063

New Zealand : +64 21 0376434

Brazil : +55 11973372647

Singapore : +65 81129229

Spain : +34 9221 33282

UAE : +971 557316937

UK : +44 330-111-DADA (3232)

Website : www.dadabhagwan.org